JAPANESE NOW

Text
Volume 1

ESTHER M. T. SATO
LOREN I. SHISHIDO
MASAKO SAKIHARA

University of Hawaii Press
Honolulu

91 90 89 88   7 6

TAPES TO ACCOMPANY THIS TEXT ARE AVAILABLE FROM
UNIVERSITY OF HAWAII PRESS
2840 KOLOWALU STREET
HONOLULU, HAWAII 96822

Library of Congress Cataloguing in Publication Data

Sato, Esther M. T., 1915–
    Japanese now.

    Contents: v. 1. Text.
    1. Japanese language—Text-books for foreigners.
I. Shishido, Loren I., 1946–   II. Sakihara, Masako,
1935–   III. Title.
PL539.3.S28   495.6'82421   81–23142
ISBN 0–8248–0773–1 (v. 1)   AACR2

CONTENTS

PREFACE

Language learning is an essential component of general education today. The series *Japanese Now* was developed with the belief that in an increasingly complex and technologically advanced world general education must encompass a realization and appreciation of the necessity for mutual interdependence and peaceful coexistence among all peoples and nations. The study of languages and cultures provides students with a means to know and understand their fellow citizens of the world. This series will introduce them to the Japanese and give them valuable insights into how the Japanese communicate and meet daily challenges and human needs.

The four volumes of this series are designed to serve as the basic unit of a four-year high school Japanese language program. In a three-year program, volume 4 may be used as a reader for advanced students. Volume 1 focuses on the individual and her friends and gives the student a basic vocabulary of useful words and expressions. Volume 2 acquaints the student with his immediate surroundings, including the family and the neighborhood. Volume 3 leads the student into the larger community and introduces him to Japanese literature and art. Volume 4 takes a broad look at Japan, its cities, history, religion, and its political and economic life. All four volumes are intended to teach language and at the same time expand and deepen the student's understanding of various aspects of Japanese culture.

The differences between colloquial and literary Japanese are clearly indicated. Students are first exposed to the spoken language as it is used daily in various social contexts, and are familiarized with the basic structure of Japanese as well. Later, the formal written style is introduced. Students will be able to contrast and compare the two styles readily.

Many people have helped us directly and indirectly in making this series a reality. The administrators, teachers, and students of the Hawaii State Department of Education have supported our efforts throughout. Without their cooperation, encouragement, and assistance, such a project would never have been attempted, much less realized. Loreen Ige, Joanne Kanda, and June Kuwabara of Castle High School, Howard Asao of Farrington High School, and Fumiyo Yamanaka of Waiakea High School used and tested our materials and made invaluable comments and suggestions for improving the final product. To the Reverend Eijo Ikenaga goes our warmest gratitude for his creative artwork and calligraphy. At the University of Hawaii, our special thanks go to the administrators and our colleagues in the College of Education, particularly those in the Department of Curriculum and Instruction and the Research and Development Group, and to colleagues in the Department of East Asian Languages: David E. Ashworth and Takako Ayusawa, who helped with editorial tasks, and Kyoko Hijirida, who assisted with the preparation of tapes. To the University of Hawaii Press, we say "mahalo" for the help and guidance we received throughout the publication process.

INTRODUCTION

The Japanese language is spoken by more than 120 million people in Japan proper and a few million more in Okinawa, Korea, and some islands of the South Pacific. Some sixteen centuries ago, the Chinese writing system was introduced in Japan and has since been used with the Japanese syllabary, which was developed in Japan. The Japanese language has many dialects, but since the Meiji Restoration in 1868, standard Japanese has been based on the Tokyo dialect. Today, the Tokyo dialect is the language spoken and understood by the majority of the people of Japan.

This series is designed to enable the student to learn Japanese by listening, speaking, reading, and writing from the beginning. No romanization is used. Students learn to pronounce and recognize the Japanese syllabary. Introducing the syllables and symbols reinforces and accelerates the language learning process. In addition, students are more likely to develop a "pure" pronunciation through the use of the syllabary, and will learn kanji more readily.

Nine introductory units provide a basic vocabulary of everyday words and useful expressions that allow the student to begin speaking Japanese immediately. Grammar and grammatical structures are not discussed in these units. While students practice greetings and basic conversations, they also practice reading and writing the kana syllabaries.

The major objective of this series is to develop not only oral fluency, but an overall competence in Japanese, which also includes insights into the cultural context of the language as well. Thus, the material presented covers all facets of Japanese life and is keyed to topics relevant to students' interests and related studies. All four volumes have Japan as the setting and build lessons around various situations and episodes that will help the student to understand and appreciate Japan and the Japanese.

NOTE ON PRONUNCIATION

Japanese is a syllabic language. It is made up of distinct syllables which have the same sound duration. Five syllables are vowels that may be short or long with the long given twice the sound duration of the short vowel:

It is important that a clear distinction is made between long and short vowels.

あ resembles *a* in f*a*ther, but is much shorter; ああ is like *aa*h.

い is equivalent to *i* in mach*i*ne, but shorter; いい sounds like *ee*k.

う resembles *ui* in s*ui*t, but is pronounced with unrounded lips; くう is like c*oo*l.

え is the same as *e* in g*e*t; えい or ええ is like *ee*h.

お is pronounced like *o* in *o*bey; おう or おお is like *oo*h.

ん is pronounced like *n* in ほんです when it is followed by た、な、ら、だ ぎょう. When it is followed by ま、ぱ、ば ぎょう it is pronounced with an m sound as in ほんも、たんぽぽ (dandelion), and ほんばこ (bookcase). In all other cases ん is prounounced like *ng* in the word si*ng*.

INTRODUCTORY UNITS

GREETINGS
VOCABULARY
EXPRESSIONS

INTRODUCTORY UNIT 1

GREETINGS

おはよう　ございます。   Good morning.
こんにちは。   Good day.
こんばんは。   Good evening.
さようなら。（じゃあね…。）   Good-bye. (See you . . .)

VOCABULARY

Nouns (names of places or things)

にほん	Japan	（お）てあらい	toilet
としょかん	library	くうこう	airport
うち	home; house	がっこう	school
うみ	beach; ocean		

Verbs (words that show action or state of being): Verbs that take へ. (Dictionary form is in parentheses.)

いきます（いく）
to go

きます（くる）
to come

かえります（かえる）
to return

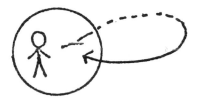

EXPRESSIONS*

にほんへ　いきます。   I am going to Japan.*
うみへ　いきます。   I am going to the beach.
くうこうへ　いきます。   I am going to the airport.
としょかんへ　いきます。   I am going to the library.
おてあらいへ　いきます。   I am going to the bathroom.
がっこうへ　きます。   I come to school.
うちへ　かえります。   I go home.
にほんへ　いきますか。   Are you going to Japan?
  ええ、いきます。   Yes, I am going.
  いいえ、いきません。   No, I'm not going.

* In Japanese sentences the -ます form of a verb can express the present or the future tense. Also, the subject pronouns, I, you, he, she, we, they, are usually omitted, but understood according to the context. Hence にほんへ　いきます may mean *I go to Japan, I'm going to Japan,* or *I will go to Japan;* or *He/She/We/They go (goes) to Japan, is (are) going to Japan,* or *will go to Japan.* For convenience, the expressions in all these introductory units are translated in the present tense with the subject pronoun I.

INTRODUCTORY UNIT 2
GREETINGS

いって　まいります or いって　きます。	I'll be going. (Used when you are leaving home or taking leave.)
いって　いらっしゃい。	(Used when someone is leaving and you are seeing him off.)
おやすみ　なさい。	Good night.

VOCABULARY

Nouns

くるま	car	かいもの	shopping
みず	water	えんぴつ	pencil
（お）すし	sushi (vinegared rice with fish and vegetables)	ごはん	meal; cooked rice
		べんきょう	study
くつ	shoes	かみ	paper
おちゃ	tea		
えいが	movie		

Verbs that take を

かいます　（かう）	to buy
たべます　（たべる）	to eat
します　（する）	to do
のみます　（のむ）	to drink
みます　（みる）	to see; to watch

EXPRESSIONS

くるまを　かいます。	I am going to buy a car.
くつを　かいます。	I am going to buy shoes.
えんぴつを　かいます。	I am going to buy a pencil.
みずを　のみます。	I am going to drink water.
おちゃを　のみます。	I am going to drink tea.
ごはんを　たべます。	I am going to eat a meal.
おすしを　たべます。	I am going to eat sushi.
えいがを　みます。	I am going to see a movie.
かいものを　します。	I am going to shop.
べんきょうを　します。	I am going to study.
くるまを　かいますか。	Are you going to buy a car?
ええ、かいます。	Yes, I am going to buy.
いいえ、かいません。	No, I'm not going to buy.

INTRODUCTORY UNIT 3

GREETINGS

ただいま。	I am home. I'm back.
おかえりなさい。	Welcome home. (Response to ただいま .)
おねがい します。	(This expression is used when requesting something or asking a favor.)

VOCABULARY

Nouns

ほん	book	にほんご	the Japanese language
ひらがな	the Japanese alphabet	おんがく	music
かたかな	the Japanese alphabet used for loanwords		

More verbs that take を

よみます（よむ）	to read	ききます（きく）	to listen; to hear
はなします（はなす）	to speak	かきます（かく）	to write
やすみます（やすむ）	to rest; to be absent		

EXPRESSIONS

ほんを よみます。	I read a book. *or* I am going to read a book.
おんがくを ききます。	I listen to music.
にほんごを はなします。	I speak Japanese.
ひらがなを かきます。	I write hiragana.
かたかなを かきます。	I write katakana.
がっこうを やすみます。	I stay away from school.
にほんごを はなしますか。	Do you speak Japanese?
ええ、はなします。	Yes, I do speak.
いいえ、はなしません。	No, I don't speak.

INTRODUCTORY UNIT 4

GREETINGS

どうぞ 。	Please.
いただきます。	I will receive. (Used before eating or drinking.)
けっこうです。	No, thank you.
ごちそうさま（でした）。	Thank you for the meal (tea, etc.). (Used after eating or drinking.)

VOCABULARY

Nouns

えいご	the English language	おかね	money	でんわ	telephone
ひま	free time	しゅくだい	homework	しけん	test
せんせい	teacher	いぬ	dog	ねこ	cat

Verbs that take が

わかります（わかる）	to understand
います（いる）	there is; there are. (Used for animate objects such as people and animals.)
かかります（かかる）	to take; to cost
あります（ある）	to have; there is; there are. (Used for inanimate objects such as books, test, shoes.)

EXPRESSIONS

えいごが　わかります。	I understand English.
でんわが　あります。	There is a telephone.
ひまが　あります。	I have free time.
しゅくだいが　あります。	I have homework.
しけんが　あります。	I have a test.
せんせいが　います。	There is the teacher.
いぬが　います。	There is a dog.
ねこが　います。	There is a cat.
おかねが　かかります。	It costs money.
えいごが　わかりますか。	Do you understand English?
ええ、わかります。	Yes, I do understand.
いいえ、わかりません。	No, I don't understand.

INTRODUCTORY UNIT 5

GREETINGS

ありがとうございました。	Thank you.
しつれい　しました。	I'm sorry to have bothered you.
ごめんなさい。	Excuse me. (Used when one has inconvenienced someone.)
どういたしまして *or* いいえ。	Don't mention it. You are welcome. Not at all.

VOCABULARY

Nouns

いま	now	おととい	the day before yesterday
あさって	the day after tomorrow	あした	tomorrow
きのう	yesterday	まいにち	every day
きょう	today		

Verbs

おきます（おきる）	to get up	ねます（ねる）	to go to bed
いいます（いう）	to say	きました	came

6

EXPRESSIONS

いま　おきます。	I am going to get up now.
いま　ねます。	I am going to go to sleep now.
いま　いいます。	I am going to say it now.
きょう　かいます。	I am going to buy it today.
あした　やすみます。	I am going to rest tomorrow.
あさって　かえります。	I am going to return home the day after tomorrow.
まいにち　いきます。	I go every day.
おととい　きましたか。	I came the day before yesterday.
きのう　みました。	I saw it yesterday.
おととい　きましたか。	Did you come the day before yesterday?
ええ、きました。	Yes, I did come.
いいえ、きませんでした。	No, I didn't come.

INTRODUCTORY UNIT 6

GREETINGS

ちょっと　しつれい。	Excuse me. Excuse me for a while.
すみません。	I'm sorry to trouble you. Excuse me. Thank you.
どうも。	Thank you. I'm sorry to have bothered you.

VOCABULARY

Adjectives (descriptive words)

あかい	red		あつい	hot
あおい	blue		くろい	black
つめたい	cold		おいしい	delicious
しろい	white		いい	good
きいろい	yellow			

Adjective + Noun

あかい　くつ	red shoes		しろい　くつ	white shoes
くろい　くつ	black shoes		あおい　えんぴつ	blue pencil
きいろい　かみ	yellow paper		おいしい　おすし	delicious sushi
つめたい　みず	cold water		あつい　おちゃ	hot tea
いい　えいが	good movie			

EXPRESSIONS

あかい　くつが　あります。	I have red shoes. There are red shoes.
しろい　くつが　あります。	I have white shoes.
くろい　くつが　あります。	I have black shoes.
あおい　えんぴつが　あります。	I have a blue pencil.
きいろい　かみが　あります。	I have yellow paper.
おいしい　おすしを　たべます。	I'll eat delicious sushi.
つめたい　みずを　のみます。	I'll drink cold water.
あつい　おちゃを　のみます。	I'll drink hot tea.
いい　えいがを　みます。	I'm going to see a good movie.

INTRODUCTORY UNIT 7

GREETINGS

あついですね。	It's hot, isn't it?
よく　ふりますねえ。	It rains a lot, doesn't it?
おでかけ　ですか。	Are you on your way out? (Used to greet a person who is going out.)

VOCABULARY

Adjectives

あつい	hot	あたらしい	new
さむい	cold (climate)	ふるい	old
おおきい	large	むずかしい	difficult
ちいさい	small	やさしい	easy

Adjective + Noun

あたらしい　くるま	new car	ふるい　くるま	old car
おおきい　うち	large house	ちいさい　うち	small house
むずかしい　しけん	hard test	やさしい　しけん	easy test

EXPRESSIONS

さむいですねえ。	It's cold, isn't it?
あたらしい　くるまを　かいます。	I'm going to buy a new car.
ふるい　くるまを　かいます。	I'm going to buy an old car.
おおきい　うちを　かいます。	I'm going to buy a large house.
ちいさい　うちを　かいます。	I'm going to buy a small house.
むずかしい　しけんが　あります。	I have a hard test.
やさしい　しけんが　あります。	I have an easy test.

INTRODUCTORY UNIT 8

GREETINGS

ごめんください。	Is anybody home? (Used when announcing oneself.)
いらっしゃいませ。	Welcome.

VOCABULARY

Adjectives

とおい	far
ちかい	near
おもしろい	interesting
つまらない	uninteresting; boring
ながい	long
みじかい	short
たかい	expensive
やすい	inexpensive

Adjectives + Noun

とおい うみ	beach far away
ながい やすみ	long vacation
おもしろい えいが	interesting movie
たかい くつ	expensive shoes
ちかい うみ	beach nearby
みじかい やすみ	short vacation
つまらない えいが	boring movie
やすい くつ	inexpensive shoes

EXPRESSIONS

とおい うみへ いきます。	I'm going to a beach far away.
ちかい うみへ いきます。	I'm going to the beach nearby.
ながい やすみが あります。	I have a long vacation.
みじかい やすみが あります。	I have a short vacation.
おもしろい えいがを みました。	I saw an interesting movie.
つまらない えいがを みました。	I saw a boring movie.
たかい くつを かいました。	I bought expensive shoes.
やすい くつを かいました。	I bought inexpensive shoes.

INTRODUCTORY UNIT 9

USEFUL EXPRESSIONS IN CLASSROOM

1. よく　わかりません。 — I don't understand very well.
2. もういちど　いってください。 — Please say it again.
3. わかりました。 — I understood.
4. ほんを　あけてください。 — Please open your book.
5. みんなで　よんでください。 — Please read it all together.
6. みんなで　いってください。 — Please say it in chorus.
7. こたえを　いってください。 — Please say the answer.
8. よく　できました。 — You did well.
9. こたえを　かいてください。 — Please write the answer.
10. ちょっと　ちがいます。 — It's incorrect.
11. しつもんが　あります。 — I have a question.
12. ゆっくり　いってください。 — Please say it slowly.
13. きこえません。 — I can't hear.
14. しずかに　してください。 — Please be quiet.
15. こっちを　みてください。 — Please look this way.
16. みえません。 — I can't see.
17. しゅくだいを　だしてください。 — Please turn in your homework.
18. わすれました。 — I forgot.
19. なまえを　かいてください。 — Please write your name.
20. しけんを　だしてください。 — Please turn in your test.
21. ちょっと　まってください。 — Please wait a minute.
22. しけんを　かえしてください。 — Please return the test.
23. かみと　えんぴつを　だしてください。 — Please take out your pencil and paper.
24. かいてください。 — Please write.
25. ほんを　とじてください。 — Please close your book.
26. おてあらいへ　いっても　いいですか。 — May I go to the restroom?

LESSONS

READING SELECTION

DIALOGUE

VOCABULARY

GRAMMAR

DRILLS

EXERCISES

LESSON 1 *Jiro Meets Tom*

Situation: Jiro and Tom meet for the first time.

I. READING SELECTION

たなかじろうさんの[1,2]うちは[3]とうきょうです。[4]　　トム・アカウさんの　うちは
ホノルルです。

Note: numbers refer to entries in Grammar section.

II. DIALOGUE　（かいわ）

たなか：　たなかじろうです。[5]　よろしく。
アカウ：　トム・アカウです。　よろしく。
たなか：　アカウさん、うちは　どこですか。[6]
アカウ：　ホノルルです。　たなかさんは？[7]
たなか：　とうきょうです。

III. VOCABULARY　（たんご）

たなかじろう	Japanese name for a male. (In Japanese the last name comes first followed by the first name.)
の	(Particle connecting two nouns.)
です	am, is. (Depending on the context, です can mean *I am, you are, he/she is, it is,* or *they are.*)
トム・アカウ	Tom Akau. (Katakana is used to write a foreigner's name, with first name first and then the last as in English. A dot "・" is placed between the first and last name.)
よろしく	How do you do? (Idiomatic expression used often in introducing oneself.)
うち	home
どこ	where
ホノルル	Honolulu, capital of Hawaii
さん	(Suffix attached either to the first name or to the last name of someone else, never to one's own name. Corresponds to the English Mr., Mrs., Miss, Ms.)
は	(Particle which indicates the topic or subject of a sentence.)
か	(Particle at the end of a sentence indicating a question.)
とうきょう	Tokyo, capital of Japan

IV. GRAMMAR　（ぶんぽう）

1. Particles. In Japanese there are many word classes, one of which is called the "particle." It comes after a word as if it were part of the word, phrase, or sentence and indicates such things as the topic or subject, object, questions, and so on.

13

2. たなかじろうさん<u>の</u> うち   Mr. Jiro Tanaka's home.

の may be defined as a genitive particle used to join two nouns. Its function is to show that the first noun characterizes the second.

3. うち<u>は</u> とうきょうです。   My home is in Tokyo.

(Noun) は (noun) です. は is a particle which follows the topic or subject that is being talked about. Here, うち is the topic and とうきょう describes the topic introduced.

4. うちは とうきょう<u>です</u>。   My home is in Tokyo.

です means something like *is, am, are.* It is the nonpast tense which can serve for present and future events with no distinction between singular and plural subjects. It generally comes at the end of a sentence.

5. たなかじろうです。   My name is Jiro Tanaka.

Omission of the topic or subject. In Japanese the topic or subject is often omitted when it is understood and obvious to both the speaker and listener.

    Ex. （わたくしは） たなかじろうです。   (I) am Jiro Tanaka.

        （わたくしのなまえは） たなかじろうです。   (My name) is Jiro Tanaka.

6. うちは とうきょうです<u>か</u>。   Do you live in Tokyo?

か is a question marker which is added to the end of a statement and changes it into a question.

    Ex. うちは とうきょうです。   I'm living in Tokyo *or*
                                        My home is in Tokyo.

       うちは とうきょうですか。   Do you live in Tokyo? *or*
                                          Is your home in Tokyo?

7. たなかさん<u>は</u>？   And what about (you) Mr. Tanaka?

Words and phrases other than the topic or subject can also be omitted. From the context it is clear that the speaker is asking where Mr. Tanaka lives. In Japanese when the speaker refers to the listener, he often uses the listener's name instead of the personal pronoun "you."

V. DRILLS

    A. Introduce yourself to the other students.

          (Name) です。   よろしく。

    B. Question-Answer

      Ex. Q: うちは どこですか。

         A: うちは (place) です。

    C. Practice the pattern (noun) の (noun) following the example.

      Ex. Student A: トム・アカウです。うちは ホノルルです。

          Student B: トム・アカウさん<u>の</u> うちは ホノルルです。

    D. Practice the dialogue using the following sequence.

      Student A: アカウさん、 うちは どこですか。

      Student B: ホノルルです。 たなかさんは？

      Student A: とうきょうです。

LESSON 2 *Deciding to Go to The Beach*

Situation: Inviting someone to go to the beach.

I.   READING SELECTION

きょう¹ たなかさんと² アカウさんは ひまです。³ うみへ⁴ いきます。⁵

II.   かいわ

たなか： アカウさん、きょう ひまですか。

アカウ： ええ、ひまです。

たなか： じゃあ、うみへ いきませんか。⁶

アカウ： いいですね。⁷ いきましょう。⁸

III.   たんご

きょう	today. (A time word usually placed before or after the topic of a sentence.)
と	and. (Particle.)
ひま	free time
うみ	beach; ocean; sea
へ	(Particle meaning to a place.)
いきます （いく）	to go; is going; will go
ええ	yes
じゃあ	Well, . . .
いきません	is not going; do not go; will not go
いきませんか	won't you go?
いい	good; fine
いいですね	that sounds good; that's fine
いきましょう	let's go

SUPPLEMENTARY VOCABULARY

がっこう	school
プール	swimming pool
やま	mountain
あした	tomorrow
あさって	day after tomorrow
ゆうえんち	playground; amusement park
かわ	river; stream
おてあらい	restroom
としょかん	library
みずうみ	lake

15

いいえ	no
こうえん	park
にほん	Japan
いま	now
じかん	time; hour; period

IV. ぶんぽう

1. <u>きょう</u>　ひまですか。　　　　　Are you free today?

In Japanese, time words or phrases are placed before or after the topic word of the sentence. When the topic word is omitted it is usually placed at the beginning of a sentence.

Ex. アカウさんは　<u>きょう</u>　ひまですか。

Is Mr. Akau free today? *or*
Are you free today, Mr. Akau?
<u>きょう</u>　ひまですか。

Are you free today?

2. たなかさん<u>と</u>　アカウさんは　うみへ　いきます。
Mr. Tanaka and Mr. Akau (will) go to the beach.

と *and* is a particle which connects two nouns or noun phrases. Unlike the English "and," however, と cannot be used to connect clauses or sentences.

3. Word order. In Japanese sentence structure, the predicate (verb or verb phrase) comes at the end of a sentence.

Ex. うちは　とうきょう<u>です</u>。　　　My home is in Tokyo.

アカウさんは　　うみへ<u>いきません</u>。　Mr. Akau is not going (will not go) to the beach.

4. うみ<u>へ</u>　いきます　　　　　　　I go to the beach.

(Place) へ (verb). へ is a particle which follows a place word or phrase. It means to go *to* a place and is used with verbs that indicate movement from one place to another, such as　いきます　*to go,* きます *to come,*　かえります *to return.*

Ex. やま<u>へ</u>　いきます。　　　　　I go *to* the mountain.

5. いきます（いく）　　　　　　　I go.

いきます　is the nonpast formal form of the verb "to go." All Japanese verbs in the nonpast formal form are characterized with a verb stem (in this case いき) plus the suffix - ます. Verbs in this form express nonpast action which, depending on the context, may be what occurs habitually or in the future.

Ex. あした　うみへ　いきます。

I'm going to the beach tomorrow.　(future)
まいにち　がっこうへ　いきます。
I go to school every day.　　　　(habitual)

いく is the informal form of the verb いきます　and is the form usually listed in the dictionary. Henceforth, this form will be referred to as the dictionary form. Each time a new verb is introduced the dictionary form will be given in parentheses with the - ます form.

6. いきませんか

Won't you go?

Wouldn't you like to go?

(Verb negative)か。 いきません is the negative nonpast formal form of いきます. The question form -ませんか is used to invite the listener to do something.

Ex. たべませんか。

Won't you eat?

Wouldn't you like to eat?

7. いいですね。

That sounds good.

The particle ね or ねえ often occurs at the end of a sentence in conversational Japanese. It is used when the speaker agrees with the listener or expects agreement. (See lesson 8.)

8. いきましょう。

いきましょう is the tentative form of the verb いきます *to go*. The English equivalent of -ましょう is "Let's do . . ."

Ex. うみへ いきましょう。

Let's go to the beach.

うちへ かえりましょう。

Let's go home.

V. DRILLS

A. Substitution

Ex. きょう ひまですか。

Cue: あした

あさって

いま

the day after tomorrow

now

tomorrow

B. Question-Answer

Ex. Q: きょう ひまですか。

A: ええ、 ひまです。

1. うちは ホノルルですか。

2. アカウさん ですか。

3. たなか じろうさん ですか。

4. うちは とうきょうですか。

C. Substitution

Ex. うみへ いきませんか。

Cue: mountain　　　　　　　pool

river　　　　　　　　Japan

amusement park　　　　restroom

school　　　　　　　library

17

D.   Question-Answer

    Ex.   Cue: beach

            Q: (Name)、<u>うみへ</u>　いきませんか。

            A: ええ、いきましょう。

    Cue: Mr. Tanaka's home

            Mr. Akau's home

            Tokyo

            Honolulu

            my home

LESSON 3 *Deciding to Go to McDonald's*

Situation: Asking someone to go to lunch.

I. READING SELECTION

たなかさんと　アカウさんは　マクドナルドで¹　おひるを²　たべます。

II. かいわ

たなか：　おひるは？³

アカウ：　まだです。

たなか：　じゃあ、　マクドナルドで　たべませんか。

アカウ：　いいですね。　たべましょう。

III. たんご

マクドナルド	McDonald's
で	at. (Particle.)
おひる	lunch
を	(Particle which marks the object of a verb.)
たべます（たべる）	to eat
まだです	not yet

SUPPLEMENTARY VOCABULARY

おふろ	bath
レストラン	restaurant
べんきょう	study
しゅくだい	homework
ごはん	meal; cooked rice
アイス・クリーム	ice cream
ケーキ	cake
きのう	yesterday
おととい	day before yesterday
のみます（のむ）	to drink
みます（みる）	to see; watch
ききます（きく）	to hear; listen
かいます（かう）	to buy
デパート	department store
なに	what

IV. ぶんぽう

1. マクドナルド<u>で</u> たべます。　　　　　　　I eat at McDonald's.

   にほん<u>で</u> べんきょうします。　　　　　　I study in Japan.

   で is a particle meaning *at* or *in* and indicates the location where action takes place.

2. おひる<u>を</u> たべます。　　　　　　　　　　I eat lunch.

   を is a particle which indicates that what precedes it is the object of the verb.

   　　Ex. ハンバーガー<u>を</u> たべます。　　　　I eat hamburger.

   　　　　　　　　　　　　　　　　　　　　　　I will eat hamburger.

   　　　　　　　　　　　　　　　　　　　　　　I am going to eat hamburger.

3. おひるは？ まだです。　　　　　　　　　　　Have you had lunch? Not yet.

   In Lesson 1 we learned that topics or subjects, or words and phrases can be omitted when the context is clear to both the speaker and listener. おひるは？ is a similar case of phrase deletion, where たべましたか *Have you eaten?* is understood and deleted. The answer まだです *not yet* is the abbreviation of まだたべていません *I have not eaten yet*.

4. Word order. Topic or subject + location + action.

   　　Ex. たなかさんは マクドナルドで ハンバーガーを たべます。

   　　　　　Mr. Tanaka eats a hamburger at McDonald's.

V. DRILLS

A. Question-Answer

   Ex. Q: <u>おひるは？</u>

   　　A: まだです。

   1. おふろは？
   2. しゅくだいは？
   3. たなかさんは？
   4. ごはんは？

B. Question-Answer

   Ex. Q: どこで たべますか。　　　　　Cue: マクドナルド

   　　A: マクドナルドで たべます。

   1. どこで べんきょうを しますか。　　　　うち
   2. どこで ほんを よみますか。　　　　　　としょかん
   3. どこで おんがくを ききますか。　　　　がっこう
   4. どこで おちゃを のみますか。　　　　　たなかさんの うち
   5. どこで くつを かいますか。　　　　　　デパート

C. Question-Answer

   Ex. Q: おひるを たべますか。

   　　A: ええ、 たべます。 or いいえ、 たべません。

   1. アイス・クリームを たべますか。
   2. ケーキを たべますか。
   3. ハンバーガーを たべますか。
   4. Continue using vocabulary from lessons.

D. Question-Answer

Ex. Q: (Name), <u>うみへ</u> いきませんか。

 A: ええ、 いきましょう。

1. としょかん
2. プール
3. にほん
4. こうえん
5. おてあらい
6. みずうみ

VI. REVIEW

A. Question-Answer

1. うちは どこですか。

2. しゅくだいは？

3. Use questions from lessons.

B. Say the following in Japanese.

1. Where is your home?

2. Won't you go to the beach?

3. Let's go to the beach.

4. mountains and ocean

5. rivers and lakes

VII. EXERCISES

A. Answer the following according to lesson 3.

1. たなかさんと アカウさんは どこへ いきますか。
2. たなかさんと アカウさんは なにを たべますか。
3. たなかさんと アカウさんは どこで たべますか。
4. たなかさんと アカウさんは マクドナルドで なにを たべますか。

LESSON 4 *Deciding What to Have for Lunch*

Situation: Deciding what to order for a meal.

I. READING SELECTION

たなかさんと　アカウさんは　マクドナルドへ　いきました。[1]　ビッグ・マックと
ポテト・フライを　たべました。　コーラを　のみました。

II. かいわ

たなか：　なにを　たべますか。

アカウ：　ビッグ・マックと　ポテト・フライを　おねがいします。

たなか：　のみものは？

アカウ：　コーラ

たなか：　じゃあ、　ここに　いてください。[2,3]　ぼくが[4]　かいますから。[5]

III. たんご

ビッグ・マック	(Big Mac is a compound foreign word written in かたかな. It has a dot between the two words.)
ポテト・フライ	potato fry (french fries)
コーラ	cola
なに	what
おねがいします	(Expression used when requesting something or asking a favor.)
のみもの	drinks
ここに　いてください	Please stay here.
が	(Particle which indicates that the word or phrase preceding it is the subject of the sentence.)
ぼく	I; me (Informal masculine usage.)
わた（く）し	I; me (Both masculine and feminine.)
から	because; since; as. (Particle.)

SUPPLEMENTARY VOCABULARY

だれ	who
います（いる）	to be
はなします（はなす）	to speak
きます（くる）	to come
かえります（かえる）	to return
します（する）	to do
よみます（よむ）	to read
かきます（かく）	to write

やすみます（やすむ）	to rest
おきます（おきる）	to wake up
ねます（ねる）	to sleep; to go to bed
いいます（いう）	to say
なまえ	name
しゅくだい	homework

IV. ぶんぽう

1. ごはんを　たべました。　　　　　　　　　I ate breakfast. (Can also mean lunch or dinner.)

   The verb stem plus ました indicates that the action took place in the past or just finished.

   Ex. うみへ　いきました。　　　　　　　　I went to the beach.

2. いてください。　　　　　　　　　　　　Please stay (remain).

   The -て form of a verb plus ください is an expression which means *please do . . .*

   Ex. たべてください。　　　　　　　　　　Please eat.

   Additional verbs in -て form.

います（いる）	いて	きます（くる）	きて
たべます（たべる）	たべて	かえります（かえる）	かえって
のみます（のむ）	のんで	します（する）	して
はなします（はなす）	はなして	よみます（よむ）	よんで
かいます（かう）	かって	かきます（かく）	かいて
ききます（きく）	きいて	ねます（ねる）	ねて
みます（みる）	みて	いいます（いう）	いって
いきます（いく）	いって	おきます（おきる）	おきて
やすみます（やすむ）	やすんで		

3. ここに　いてください。　　　　　　　　　Please stay here.

   …に　います　　…に　あります

   A place word or phrase followed by particle に expresses the location of someone or something. In the case of an animated being the verb following should be います. In the case of an inanimate object the verb should be あります.

   Ex. ここに　いぬが　います。　　　　　There is a dog here.

   　　アカウさんは　どこに　いますか。　Where is Mr. Akau?

   　　ここに　ほんが　あります。　　　　There is (are) a book(s) here.

4. ぼくが　かいます。　　　　　　　　　　I will buy.

   が is a particle which indicates that what precedes it is the subject of the sentence. It is used when the subject of the sentence needs to be emphasized and made clear. In English this is accomplished by stress.

   Ex. (Subject) が (verb)

   　　ぼくが　かいます。　　　　　　　　I will buy.

   　　　　　　　　　　　　　　　　　　　I am going to buy.

23

5. ここに　いてください。　ぼくが　かいますから。

Please stay here. I will (go) and buy it.

から is a particle which means *because, since,* or *as.* It follows a clause or a sentence that shows some cause or reason for another statement. In conversation the order of the statements is often reversed.

Ex. ぼくが　かいますから　ここに　いてください。

Because I will buy it, please stay here.

ここに　いてください。　ぼくが　かいますから。

Please stay here. I will go and buy it.

V. DRILLS

A. Repeat and give the English equivalent for the following:

1. いてください。

2. のんでください。

3. きてください。

4. はなしてください。

5. かってください。

6. きいてください。

7. みてください。

B. Question-Answer

Ex. Q: たなかさんが　かいますか。

Cue: ぼく

A: いいえ、　ぼくが　かいます。

1. たなかさんが　いきますか。
   Cue: わたくし

2. たなかさんが　きますか。
   Cue: アカウさん

3. アカウさんが　しますか。
   Cue: たなかさん

4. アカウさんが　かきますか。
   Cue: ぼく

5. たなかさんが　はなしますか。
   Cue: アカウさん

6. アカウさんが　いいますか。
   Cue: わたくし

7. アカウさんが　よみますか。
   Cue: たなかさん

C. SUBSTITUTION

Ex. ここにいて　ください。

Cue: 1. がっこう　　　3. マクドナルド　　　5. うち

2. うみ　　　4. レストラン　　　6. アカウさんの　うち

24

D. Complete the following with the given nouns and verbs in the - て form.

Ex. _____ を _____ ください。

Cue: (ハンバガー)　　(たべる)

　　__ハンバガー__ を　__たべて__ください。

1. (コーラ)　(のむ)
2. (にほんご)　(はなす)
3. (レコード)　(きく)
4. (ほん)　(よむ)
5. (なまえ)　(かく)
6. (しゅくだい)　(する)
7. (くつ)　(かう)

VI. EXERCISE

A. Answer the following questions according to the dialogue:

1. アカウさんと　たなかさんは　いま　どこに　いますか。
2. アカウさんは　なにを　たべましたか。
3. アカウさんは　なにを　のみましたか。
4. だれが　コーラを　のみましたか。
5. だれが　かいましたか。
6. いま　だれと　だれが　マクドナルドに　いますか。

B. Write a brief paragraph describing a situation in which you and a friend have gone somewhere and have had lunch together. Using your paragraph, create a dialogue in which the two people involved discuss where they are going and what they will be eating.

LESSON 5 *Jiro and Tom Decide to Go to the Movies*

Situation: Asking someone if he would like to go to the movies.

I. READING SELECTION

アカウくんと　たなかくんは　ひまです。えいがに¹　いきます。　ちゃんばらを
みます。

II. かいわ

たなか：　これから　いそがしいですか。

アカウ：　いいえ、べつに…

たなか：　じゃあ、えいがに　いきませんか。

アカウ：　いいですね。

たなか：　なにを　みましょうか。²

アカウ：　そうですねえ…。

たなか：　ちゃんばらが　いいですか、せいぶげきが　いいですか。³

アカウ：　ちゃんばらに　しましょう。⁴

III. たんご

くん	(Masculine usage for　さん, used generally for one's peers or males younger than oneself.)
えいが	movie
ちゃんばら	sword fighting in samurai movies
に	to. (Particle used with verbs of direction いきます,　きます, and so on.)
これから	from now
いそがしい	busy
いいえ、べつに	no, not especially
みましょうか	shall we see . . . ?
そうですねえ…	let's see . . .
せいぶげき	cowboy movies
…に　しましょう	let's decide on . . .

SUPPLEMENTARY VOCABULARY

サンドウィッチ	sandwich
おんがく	music

26

IV. ぶんぽう

1. えいが<u>に</u>　<u>いきません</u><u>か</u>。　　　　　Wouldn't you like to go to the movies?

(Noun) に (motion verb). The particle に instead of へ is more commonly used with motion verbs いきます；きます，and　かえります　when the word preceding it is not a place noun. Place nouns can be followed by either に or へ . Compare the following:

Ex.　えいが<u>に</u>　<u>いきます</u>。　　　　　I'm going to the movies.

　　　かいもの<u>に</u>　<u>いきます</u>。　　　　I'm going to shop.

　　　うち<u>へ</u>　<u>かえります</u>。　　　　　I'm returning home.

2. なにを　<u>みましょう</u><u>か</u>。　　　　　What shall we see?

In lesson 2, the verb stem plus ましょう was translated as *Let's* . . . . (See note 8.) By adding the question particle か the meaning is changed to *Shall we* . . . ?

3. ちゃんばらが　いいです<u>か</u>、せいぶげきが　いいです<u>か</u>。

Would you like to see a sword-fighting samurai movie or a western?

When giving choices for an answer, the alternatives are listed …か、…か as many times as there are choices. Each choice is marked off with " 、 " which is used like the English comma. Both clauses before か should end with the formal verb endings - ます or - ました, or the copula です (でした).

Ex. きょう　いきます<u>か</u>、あした　いきます<u>か</u>。

　　Are you going today or tomorrow?

　　コーラが　いいです<u>か</u>、ジュースが　いいです<u>か</u>、コーヒーが　いいです<u>か</u>。

　　Will you have cola, juice, or coffee?

　　うみへ　いきました<u>か</u>、えいがに　いきました<u>か</u>。

　　Did you go to the beach or to the movies?

4. ちゃんばら<u>に</u>　<u>しましょう</u>。　　　　　Let's decide on *chambara*.

(Noun) に　します。The verb します means *to do*, but the phrase に　します means *to decide on*.

Ex. a.　Q:　なにを　みましょうか。　　　What shall we see?
　　　　A:　ちゃんばらを　みましょう。or　Let's see *chambara*.

　　　　A:　ちゃんばらに　しましょう。　　Let's decide on *chambara*.

　　b.　Q:　どこへ　いきましょうか。　　Where shall we go?
　　　　A:　ワイキキへ　いきましょう。or　Let's go to Waikiki.

　　　　A:　ワイキキに　しましょう。　　Let's decide on Waikiki.

27

V. DRILLS

A. Say the following in Japanese.

Ex. Shall we go today or tomorrow?

きょう　いきましょうか、あした　いきましょうか。

1. Shall we study at home or at the library?
2. Shall we eat hamburgers or sandwiches?
3. Shall we watch television or read a book?

B. Question-Answer. Answer the following according to the example using both forms.

Ex. Q: なにを　たべましょうか。

A: ハンバーガーに　しましょう or ハンバーガーを　たべましょう。

1. なにを　みましょうか。　　　　　ちゃんばら
2. なにを　のみましょうか。　　　　コーラ
3. どこへ　いきましょうか。　　　　としょかん
4. どこで　たべましょうか。　　　　マクドナルド

C. Give the Japanese equivalent to the following sentences using the different forms shown in the example.

Ex. I eat sushi.　　　　　　　　おすしを　たべます。

Do you eat sushi?　　　　　おすしを　たべますか。

I do not eat sushi.　　　　おすしを　たべません。

Won't you eat sushi?　　　おすしを　たべませんか。

I ate sushi.　　　　　　　　おすしを　たべました。

Did you eat sushi?　　　　おすしを　たべましたか。

1. I drink juice.
2. I see a movie.
3. I listen to music.
4. I read a book.

28

LESSON 6 *Jiro Prefers to Study for the Test*

Situation: Declining an invitation.

I. READING SELECTION

アカウくんは　あたらしい　レコードを　かいました。　でも、　たなかくんは
いそがしいです。あさって　えいごの　しけんが　ありますから、しけんの
べんきょうを　します。

II. かいわ

くるま

あした　New York　へ　いきたちが せんが

アカウ：　あたらしい　レコードを　かいました。　ききますか。

たなか：　いまは　だめです。

アカウ：　どうして？[1]

あした

たなか：　えいごの　しけんが　あります。[2]

アカウ：　しけんは　あさってでしょう？[3]

たなか：　ええ、　でも…　そうです

アカウ：　じゃあ、　がんばって…。[4]

III. たんご

あたらしい	new
レコード	record
えいご	English
しけん	test
いまは　だめです。	not right now
だめ	no good
どうして	why
あります　(ある)	there is; (I) have
でしょう	isn't it? (Used with rising intonation.)
でも	but
がんばって	give it all you've got; hang in there

SUPPLEMENTARY VOCABULARY

ふるい	old
おもしろい	interesting
あかい	red
たかい	expensive
くるま	car
にほんご	Japanese language
アメリカ	United States

タイプライター	typewriter
ざっし	magazine
カメラ	camera
おかね	money
セール	bargain sale
デート	date (to have a date)
えんぴつ	pencil
ペン	pen
ノート	notebook
でんわ	telephone
けしごむ	eraser
いす	chair
つくえ	desk
つめたい	cold
おいしい	delicious
すし	sushi
なに	what
テープ	tape
テレビ	television
ジュース	juice

IV. ぶんぽう

1. どうして (だめですか)?   Why?

   According to the context, what follows どうして is understood and is omitted here.

2. しけん<u>が</u> <u>あります</u>。   I have a test.

   あります is the nonpast formal form of the verb "to be; to exist." It does not take an object and is usually translated as *there is; there are*. しけんがあります literally means *there is a test,* but is translated here as *I have a test*.

3. しけんは あさって <u>でしょう</u>?   The test is the day after tomorrow, isn't it?

   でしょう is the tentative form of です. With rising intonation it becomes a question.

4. じゃあ、がんばって 。   Give it all you've got, then.

   ください in conjunction with the -て form meaning *please do . . .* is often dropped in an informal conversation with peers.

30

V. DRILLS

A. Substitution

1. <u>あたらしい</u>　レコードを　かいました。

   a. old

   b. good

   c. interesting

2. ＿＿＿＿＿＿＿　ほんを　よみました。

   a. new

   b. old

   c. good

   d. interesting

3. ＿＿＿＿＿＿＿　くるまが　あります。

   a. new

   b. old

   c. red

   d. expensive

   e. good

B. Say the following in Japanese.

Ex. English test　えいごの　しけん

1. Japanese test
2. American car
3. Japanese car
4. American typewriter
5. I have an English book.

6. He has a Japanese book.
7. We bought American magazines.
8. They read Japanese magazines.
9. Did you buy a Japanese camera?
10. Did you see an American camera?

C. Say the following in Japanese.

Ex. There is a telephone. <u>でんわ</u>が　あります。

1. There is a test.
2. There is free time.
3. There is a sale.
4. I have homework.
5. There is a mountain.

D. Question-Answer

Ex. Q.　なにが　ありますか。　　　　Cue: ほん

A.　<u>ほん</u>が　あります。

31

1. えんぴつ   5. けしごむ
2. ペン   6. いす
3. ノート   7. つくえ
4. でんわ

E. Substitution

Ex. しけんは　あさってでしょう？

Cue: 1. しけんは　あした
2. うちは　とうきょう
3. きょうは　ひま
4. おひるは　まだ
5. いまは　だめ

F. Question-Answer

Ex. Q: なにを　かいましたか。   Cue: (new record)
    A: あたらしい　レコードを　かいました。

1. なにを　のみましたか。   (cold water)
2. なにを　みましたか。   (sword-fighting movie)
3. どこへ　いきましたか。   (Tokyo)
4. なにを　たべましたか。   (delicious sushi)
5. どこで　よみましたか。   (library)
6. なにが　ありましたか。   (red car)
7. どこで　かいましたか。   (department store)

VI. REVIEW

Answer the following appropriately.

A. Ex. Q: どこへ　いきますか。   A: <u>がっこうへ</u>　いきます。
     1. なにを　しますか。
     2. なにを　たべますか。
     3. なにを　のみますか。

B. Ex. Q: えいがが　いいですか、テレビが　いいですか。   A: テレビを　みましょう。
     1. ちゃんばらが　いいですか、せいぶげきが　いいですか。
     2. コーラが　いいですか、ジュースが　いいですか。
     3. やまが　いいですか、うみが　いいですか。
     4. レコードが　いいですか、テープが　いいですか。

C. Ex. Q: おひるは？   A: まだです。
    1. べんきょうは？
    2. ごはんは？
    3. しゅくだいは？
    4. おふろは？

VII. EXERCISE

Answer the questions according to the dialogue.

1. アカウさんは　なにを　かいましたか。
2. たなかさんは　いま　レコードを　ききますか。
3. たなかさんは　いま　どうして　レコードを　ききませんか。
4. なんの　しけんが　ありますか。
5. しけんは　あしたですか。

LESSON 7 *Jiro Buys a Birthday Present*

Situation: Shopping.

I. READING SELECTION

たなかくんは　おとうさんの　たんじょうびの　プレゼントを　かいました。

ハンカチと　くつしただけ　かいました。

II. かいわ

アカウ：　それは　なんですか。[1]

たなか：　これ[2]ですか。　たんじょうびの　プレゼントです。

アカウ：　だれの　たんじょうびですか。

たなか：　ちちの　たんじょうびです。

アカウ：　なにを　かいましたか。

たなか：　くつしたと　ハンカチです。[3]

アカウ：　それだけですか。[4]

たなか：　そう、それだけです。

III. たんご

おとうさん	father. (Used to refer to someone else's father or to your own among family members.)
たんじょうび	birthday
プレゼント	present
くつした	socks
ハンカチ	handkerchief
だけ	only
それ	that
なん	what
これ	this
だれの	whose
ちち	my father. (Used to refer to speaker's father when speaking to someone outside of the family.)
それだけ	that's all
そう	that's right

SUPPLEMENTARY VOCABULARY

あれ	that one over there
タワー	tower
どれ	which
なにご	what language?

34

IV. ぶんぽう

1. それは　<u>なん</u>ですか。　　　　　　　　What is that?

   Both なん and なに mean *what*. なん is used before words which begin with the sounds *t*, *d*, or *n*, and also in a compound word designating how many.

   Ex. <u>なに</u>を　かいましたか。　　　　　What did you buy?

   　　<u>なん</u>と　<u>なに</u>を　かいましたか。　What and what did you buy?

2. これ *this*; それ *that*; あれ *that over there*; どれ *which*

   これ indicates something close to the speaker, それ refers to something close to the listener, and あれ something at a distance from both the speaker and the listener. どれ is a question word. These words are demonstratives used to point at or refer to a thing or things.

3. くつしたと　ハンカチです。　　　　　　I bought socks and handkerchiefs.

   In this context, the verb is understood to be かいました and need not be repeated. Here です replaces をかいました。

   Ex. Q: なにを　<u>かいました</u>か。　　　　What did you buy?

   　　A: くつしたと　ハンカチ { <u>を　かいました。</u>　I bought socks and handkerchiefs.

   　　　　　　　　　　　　　　　　　{ です。

4. それ<u>だけ</u>ですか。　　　　　　　　　Is that all you bought?

   だけ is a particle meaning *only*.

V. DRILLS

A. Question Answer: Use of これ and それ.

   Ex. Q: それは　なんですか。　　　Cue: プレゼント
   　　A: これは　<u>プレゼント</u>です。

   1. コーラ　　　　　　　　4. おかね
   2. ハンバーガー　　　　　5. おすし
   3. カメラ　　　　　　　　6. くつしたと　ハンカチ

B. Use of あれ

   Ex. Q: あれは　なんですか。　　Cue: ゆうえんち
   　　A: あれは　<u>ゆうえんち</u>です。

   1. デパート
   2. としょかん
   3. くうこう
   4. とうきょう　タワーです。

35

C. Answer the following questions using だけです .

Ex. Q: なにが　ありますか。　　　　　　Cue:　only a book

A: ほんだけです。

1. だれが　きましたか。　　　　　　(only Mr. Tanaka)
2. だれが　いますか。　　　　　　　(only Tom and Jiro)
3. まいにち　しけんが　ありますか。　(only today and tomorrow)

D. Construct questions to the following answers

Ex. A: ちちの　たんじょうびです。
    Q: だれの　たんじょうびですか。

1. たなかさんの　うちです。
2. アカウさんの　くるまです。
3. ちちの　くつしたです。
4. せんせいの　つくえです。
5. じろうさんの　タイプライターです。

VI. EXERCISE

Respond by using だけ

1. Mr. Tanaka goes shopping and returns with a small package. You look into his package and ask him if that was all he bought. And he replies:

2. You peer into a room. You are asked how many people are in there. You see only one person, Mr. Tanaka, you respond:

3. You ask someone to do some things for you. After an hour you return to find that little has been done. You react:

4. Your friend has had lunch with a teacher. You assume that he has had a big meal. He says that he only had a hamburger.

5. Mr. Tanaka's friend comes to visit. You speak English to him. He doesn't respond. Mr. Tanaka says that he speaks only Japanese. You sigh and say "Only Japanese?"

LESSON 8 *In the Morning*

Situation: At breakfast.

I. READING SELECTION

トムくんは　はやおきですから　もう　あさごはんを　たべました。　じろうくんは
いまから　たべます。　きょうは　あついですから　トムくんと　じろうくんは
うみへ　いきます。

II. かいわ

たなか：　おはよう。　あさから　あついですねえ。

アカウ：　そうですね。[1]　うみへ　いきたい[2]ですね。

たなか：　いきましょうか。　じゃあ、　はやく[3]あさごはんを　たべましょう。

アカウ：　もう　すみました。

たなか：　え、　もう　たべました[4]か。

おかあさん：　アカウさんは　はやおきですからね。

III. たんご

はやおき	early riser
もう	already
あさごはん	breakfast
あつい	hot
おはよう	Good morning.
あさ	morning
から　(あさから)	from (from morning)
そうですね	yes, it is; that's right
いきたい	I want to go
はやく	quickly
すみます　(すむ)	to finish; to complete
え	oh?
おかあさん	mother. (Used to refer to someone else's mother or to your own among family members.)

SUPPLEMENTARY VOCABULARY

そうじ	cleaning
(お)とうばん	monitor
はは	my mother

37

IV. ぶんぽう

1. そうです is used in answer to a question.

あついですね。 ね is used when agreement is expected from the listener.

Compare the following:

Ex. A: うちは　とうきょうですか。   Is your home in Tokyo?
    B: ええ、そうです。   Yes, it is.

    A: あついですね。   It's hot, isn't it?
    B: そうですね。   Yes, it is.

2. うみへ　いきたいです。   I want to go to the beach.

The verb stem plus たい is used to express the desire of the speaker.

3. はやく　あさごはんを　たべましょう。   Let's eat breakfast quickly.

はやい	quick	はやく	quickly; early
いい	good	よく	well

The -い ending of an adjective is changed to く to form an adverb.

はやく　おきました。   I woke up early.
よく　できました。   You did well.

4. もう　たべました。   I ate already.

When used with verbs in both the nonpast and past tense, もう means *already*. It is an adverb.

もう　かえりましょう。   Let's go home already.
もう　しゅくだいを　しましたか。   Have you done your homework already?

V. DRILLS

A. Respond to the following questions with one of the answers given.

Ex. Q: あさごはんは　もう　すみましたか。

A: ええ、もう　すみました。 or いいえ、まだです。

1. しけんは　もう　すみましたか。
2. そうじは　もう　すみましたか。
3. おひるは　もう　すみましたか。
4. しゅくだいは　もう　すみましたか。

B. Say the following in Japanese.

1. Let's hurry (go quickly).
2. Let's eat quickly.
3. Let's do it quickly.
4. Please come early.
5. Let's go home early.

38

C. Change the -ます form to the - たい form with です and give the English equivalent.

    Ex. いきます   いきたいです。   I want to go.

    1. たべます

    2. みます

    3. ききます

    4. のみます

    5. します

VI. REVIEW

A. Give the Japanese equivalents for the following verbs using the different forms shown in the example.

    Ex. to eat （たべる）

Let's eat.	たべましょう。
Won't you eat?	たべませんか。
I eat.	たべます。
I do not eat.	たべません。
I ate.	たべました。

    1. to go

    2. to study

    3. to see

    4. to drink

    5. to buy

    6. to listen

LESSON 9 *Preparing to Go Swimming*

Situation: Getting ready to go swimming.

I. READING SELECTION

たなかくんと　アカウくんは　うみへ　いきます。　うみは　とおいです。

でんしゃで¹　いきます。　ろくじごろ　かえります。

II. かいわ

たなか：	みずぎは？
アカウ：	もう　いれました。
たなか：	タオルは？
アカウ：	まだです。
たなか：	はやく、はやく、でんしゃに²　おくれますよ。³
おかあさん：	おかねは？
たなか：	さんぜんえん　あります。⁴
アカウ：	ぼくも⁵　ごせんえん　あります。
おかあさん：	かえりは　なんじですか。
たなか：	ろくじ⁶　ごろ　でしょう。⁷
たなか：	いってきます。
アカウ：	いってまいります。
おかあさん：	いっていらっしゃい。　きをつけて…。

III. たんご

ガえばて

とおい	far away
でんしゃ	electric train
で	by means of. (Particle.)
ろくじ	6 o'clock
ごろ	about
みずぎ	swimwear
いれました（いれる）	put in
タオル	towel
おくれます（おくれる）	to be late
おかね	money
えん（さんぜんえん）	yen (3,000 yen)
も	also; too. (Particle.)
かえり	return
なんじ	what time?

でしょう	probably
いってまいります or いってきます	I'll be going; I'll be on my way.
いっていらっしゃい	(Expression used when someone is leaving the house. Used in response to いってまいります。)
きをつけて	be careful.

SUPPLEMENTARY VOCABULARY

れんしゅう	practice
しあい	game
じかん	hour; period
クラス	class
かていか	home economics
れきし	history
たいいく	physical education
しゃかいか	social studies
びじゅつ	art
すうがく	mathematics
かがく	science
バスケット	basketball
フット・ボール	football
テニス	tennis

COUNTING

いち	1	じゅうしち / なな	17
に	2	じゅうはち	18
さん	3	じゅうく / きゅう	19
し / よん	4	にじゅう	20
ご	5	さんじゅう	30
ろく	6	よんじゅう	40
しち / なな	7	ごじゅう	50
はち	8	ろくじゅう	60
きゅう / く	9	しち / ななじゅう	70
じゅう	10	はちじゅう	80
じゅういち	11	きゅうじゅう	90
じゅうに	12	ひゃく	100
じゅうさん	13	にひゃく	200
じゅうし / よん	14	さんびゃく	300
じゅうご	15	よんひゃく	400
じゅうろく	16	ごひゃく	500

ろっぴゃく	600	よんまん	40,000
ななひゃく	700	ごまん	50,000
はっぴゃく	800	ろくまん	60,000
きゅうひゃく	900	ななまん	70,000
せん	1,000	はちまん	80,000
にせん	2,000	きゅうまん	90,000
さんぜん	3,000	じゅうまん	100,000
よんせん	4,000	にじゅうまん	200,000
ごせん	5,000	さんじゅうまん	300,000
ろくせん	6,000	よんじゅうまん	400,000
ななせん	7,000	ごじゅうまん	500,000
はっせん	8,000	ろくじゅうまん	600,000
きゅうせん	9,000	ななじゅうまん	700,000
いちまん	10,000	はちじゅうまん	800,000
にまん	20,000	きゅうじゅうまん	900,000
さんまん	30,000	ひゃくまん	1,000,000

TIME - （じ）

なんじ	What time is it?	しちじ	7 o'clock
いちじ	1 o'clock	はちじ	8 o'clock
にじ	2 o'clock	くじ	9 o'clock
さんじ	3 o'clock	じゅうじ	10 o'clock
よじ	4 o'clock	じゅういちじ	11 o'clock
ごじ	5 o'clock	じゅうにじ	12 o'clock
ろくじ	6 o'clock		

YEN - えん

ひゃくえん	100 yen	よんせんえん	4,000 yen
にひゃくえん	200 yen	ごせんえん	5,000 yen
さんびゃくえん	300 yen	ろくせんえん	6,000 yen
よんひゃくえん	400 yen	ななせんえん	7,000 yen
ごひゃくえん	500 yen	はっせんえん	8,000 yen
ろっぴゃくえん	600 yen	きゅうせんえん	9,000 yen
ななひゃくえん	700 yen	いちまんえん	10,000 yen
はっぴゃくえん	800 yen	じゅうまんえん	100,000 yen
きゅうひゃくえん	900 yen	ひゃくまんえん	1,000,000 yen
せんえん	1,000 yen	いっせんまんえん	10,000,000 yen
にせんえん	2,000 yen	いちおくえん	100,000,000 yen
さんぜんえん	3,000 yen	じゅうおくえん	1,000,000,000 yen

IV. ぶんぽう

1. でんしゃ<u>で</u> いきます。   I'll go by train.

   でんしゃで *by means of an electric train.* で indicates the means by which an action is accomplished.

2. でんしゃ<u>に</u> <u>おくれます。</u>   You'll miss the train.

   The verb おくれます means *to miss* or *to be late* and takes the particle に after a noun.

3. でんしゃに おくれます<u>よ</u>。

   よ is an emphatic particle used at the end of a sentence to give emphasis to what you are saying.

4. <u>さんぜんえん</u> あります。   I have 3,000 yen.

   さんぜんえん is a quantity word and never takes a particle after it.

5. ぼく<u>も</u> ごせんえん あります。   I also have 5,000 yen.

   も *also; too* is a particle which can replace は, が or を.

   Ex.   ぼく<u>は</u> ごせんえん あります。   I have 5,000 yen.

          ぼく<u>も</u> ごせんえん あります。   I also have 5,000 yen.

          レコード<u>を</u> かいました。   I bought a record.

          レコード<u>も</u> かいました。   I bought a record, too.

          トムさん<u>が</u> きました。   Tom came.

          トムさん<u>も</u> きました。   Tom came, too.

6. ろくじ <u>ごろ</u>   about 6 o'clock

   ごろ means *about* or *approximate time* and follows time words which indicate a specific time.

   Ex.   よじ <u>ごろ</u> かえります。   I'll be back about 4 o'clock.

7. ろくじごろ <u>でしょう</u>。   It will probably be about 6 o'clock.

   でしょう with a rising intonation means *isn't it?* (See lesson 6.) Here it is pronounced without the rising intonation and means *probably.* It is less positive than です.

V. DRILLS

A. Substitution

     Ex.   <u>ピアノの れんしゅう</u>に おくれました。

     Cue: 1.   バスケットの れんしゅう

            2.   かていかの クラス

            3.   たいいくの じかん

            4.   すうがくの クラス

            5.   フット・ボールの しあい

            6.   テニスの しあい

            7.   れきしの クラス

            8.   しゃかいかの じかん

            9.   おんがくの じかん

          10.   かがくの じかん

B. Answer the following questions with the given cue:

Ex. Q: <u>なんじごろ</u>　いきましたか。　　　About what time did you go?

Cue:　about 6:00

A: <u>ろくじごろ</u>　いきました。

1. なんじごろ　きましたか。　　　About what time did you come?

Cue:　about　7:00

about 12:00

about　8:00

2. なんじごろ　いきましょうか。　　　About what time shall we go?

Cue:　about 10:00

about　5:00

about　4:00

3. なんじごろ　かえりましたか。　　　About what time did you return?

Cue:　about　9:00

about 11:00

about　7:00

LESSON 10 *Jiro Plans for a Date*

Situation: Planning for a date.

I. READING SELECTION

たなか　じろうくんは　きょう　メリーさんと　デートを　します。でも、じろう

くんは　おかねが　あまりありません。えいがは　おかねが　かかりますから、

じろうくんは　こまりました。

II. かいわ

おねえさん：　きょうは　なあに？[1]

じろう：　　　デート。

おねえさん：　だれと？[2]

じろう：　　　メリーさんと。

おねえさん：　そう？

じろう：　　　ねえ、おねえさん、[3]いい　とこ　しっていますか。[4]　　しりません

おねえさん：　えいがは　どう？　いま、いい　えいがを　やっていますよ。[5]

じろう：　　　でも、おかねが　かかります[6]から…。[7]

おねえさん：　けちねえ…。

III. たんご

メリー	Mary
と	with
デートします	to have a date; to go on a date
あまり	not much. (Used with negative verbs.)
かかります（かかる）	to cost
こまりました（こまる）	was troubled
ねえ	(Address particle used to get someone's attention.)
おねえさん	older sister
とこ（ところ）	place
しっています	know
どう	how about . . . ?
やっています	is playing; is doing; is having
けち	tightwad; cheapskate

SUPPLEMENTARY VOCABULARY

あね	my older sister
やきゅう	baseball
バレーボール	volleyball
ゴルフ	golf
サッカー	soccer

45

IV. ぶんぽう

1. なあに？　　　　　　　　　　　　What? (Here, it implies "What are you going to do?")

    In spoken Japanese, なに is often pronounced なあに by female speakers and children.

2. In conversation です or ですか is omitted to make it informal.

    Ex.　だれと　ですか。　　　　　だれと？

    　　そうですか。　　　　　　　そう？

    　　えいがは　どうですか。　　えいがは　どう？

    　　けちですねえ。　　　　　　けちねえ。

3. ねえ、おねえさん…　　　　　　　Look sis . . .

    The particle ねえ is a starting word used to get the listener's attention.

4. しっていますか。　　　　　　　　Do you know?

    しっています　means *I know* and is the result of an action—that I have come to know. The combination of the -て form of the verb and います is used to express an action in progress or going on now, or state of being or existence at present.

5. いい　えいがを　やっています。　　A good film is showing; being shown.

    やっています　*to perform; to act; to play* is used in discussing sports like playing baseball, football, and so on.

    Ex.　やきゅうを　やっています。　I am playing baseball.

6. おかねが　かかります。　　　　　It costs money.

    かかります　*to take (time); to take money (to cost)* does not take an object. Therefore, it does not take the object marker を. It takes the subject particle が after the noun.

7. おかねが　かかりますから。　　　Because it costs money.

    A clause which ends in から *since; because* usually indicates the reason on the speaker's part for that which he "doesn't want to," "need not" or "cannot" do stated in the clause that follows. Here, what follows から is understood and is omitted.

V. DRILLS

A. Change the informal to the formal style.

   Ex.　うちは　どこ？　　　うちは　どこですか。

   1. きょう　ひま？　　　　　　9. これ？
   2. いいね。　　　　　　　　　10. だれの　たんじょうび？
   3. のみものは　コーラ。　　　11. くつしたと　ハンカチ。
   4. これから　いそがしい？　　12. それだけ？
   5. ちゃんばらが　いい？　　　13. そう、それだけ。
   6. いまは　だめ。　　　　　　14. あついね。
   7. どうして？　　　　　　　　15. かえりは　なんじ？
   8. それ、なに？

46

B. Give the Japanese equivalent.

Ex. A good show is playing. いい　えいがを　やっています。

  1. He is reading a book.

  2. I am doing my homework.

  3. They are talking.

  4. We are watching television.

  5. She is writing.

  6. He is sleeping.

C. Give an informal answer to the questions by deleting です.

Ex. Q: それは　なんですか。　　　　Cue:　(birthday present)

    A: たんじょうびの　プレゼント。

  1. うちは　どこですか。　　　　　　(Honolulu)

  2. かえりは　なんじですか。　　　　(about 6 o'clock)

  3. どこですか。　　　　　　　　　　(McDonald's)

  4. だれですか。　　　　　　　　　　(Tom and Jiro)

  5. あれは　なんですか。　　　　　　(library)

  6. どこへ　いきますか。　　　　　　(beach)

  7. なにを　たべますか。　　　　　　(hamburger)

  8. なにを　かいましたか。　　　　　(stockings and a handkerchief)

  9. なにを　のみますか。　　　　　　(coke)

 10. だれと　うみへ　いきましたか。　(Jiro)

D. Respond to the following:

  a. in a complete sentence.

  b. with an informal answer.

  Ex. だれと　うみへ　いきましたか。

  a. メリーさんと　いきました。　　　b. メリーさんと。

  1. だれと　かいものに　いきますか。

  2. だれと　えいがに　いきますか。

  3. だれと　がっこうに　いきますか。

  4. だれと　おひるを　たべますか。

VI. EXERCISE

A. Create a dialogue about places you can go on a date that do not cost very much money.

B. What would you say in the following situations?

  1. you are leaving the house

  2. someone else is leaving the house and you are seeing him off

  3. you tell someone to be careful

  4. you are already through

LESSON 11 *Jiro Meets Mary on a Date*

Situation: Deciding where to go on a date.

I. READING SELECTION

じろうくんは　メリーさんと　デートを　します。きょうは　どうぶつえんに
しましたが、¹　ほんとうは　じろうくんは　あまり　きょうみが　ありません。

II. かいわ

<table>
<tbody>
<tr><td>じろう：</td><td>あ、　メリーさん、　こっちですよ。</td></tr>
<tr><td>メリー：</td><td>あ、　じろうさん、　おはよう。　いい　おてんきですね。</td></tr>
<tr><td>じろう：</td><td>ええ、　きょうは　どこに　しましょうか。</td></tr>
<tr><td>メリー：</td><td>そうですねえ。</td></tr>
<tr><td>じろう：</td><td>えいがを　みましょうか。うちへ　きましょうか</td></tr>
<tr><td>メリー：</td><td>ねえ、　それより　どうぶつえんへ　いきましょうよ。²</td></tr>
<tr><td>じろう：</td><td>どうぶつえん？　やきゅう　の　しあいに</td></tr>
<tr><td>メリー：</td><td>いやですか。</td></tr>
<tr><td>じろう：</td><td>いいですよ。</td></tr>
</tbody>
</table>

III. たんご

どうぶつえん	zoo
が	but. (Particle used to connect two statements.)
ほんとうは	actually
きょうみ	interest
ありません	don't have
あ、	oh; hey
こっちですよ	over here
いい　おてんきですね	It's a nice day, isn't it?
(お)てんき	(good) weather
そうですねえ	let's see
それより	instead of that
いやですか	Don't you like it?　Do you find it unpleasant?
いやです	I don't like it.
いいですよ	It's all right.

IV. ぶんぽう

1. どうぶつえんに　しましたが、ほんとうは　じろうくんは　あまり　きょうみが　ありません。

They decided on the zoo, but actually Jiro wasn't too interested in it.

(Statement) が (statement). が is a particle meaning *but* and connects two statements.

2. <u>それより、</u>　どうぶつえんへ　<u>いきましょうよ。</u>

Let's go to the zoo instead.

それより is used to give an alternative to what is suggested.

V. DRILLS

A. Say the following in Japanese.

Ex.　Instead of that, let's see a western.

それより、　せいぶげきを　みましょう。

1. Instead of that, let's go to the beach.

2. Instead of that one, let's buy this one.

3. Instead of that, let's eat hamburgers.

4. Instead of that, let's decide on this.

B. Respond to the questions by beginning with それより

Ex.　Q: ハンバーガーを　たべましょうか。

　　　A: それより　おすしを　たべましょう。

1. ちゃんばらを　みましょうか。

2. ほんを　よみましょうか。

3. おちゃを　のみましょうか。

4. にほんごを　はなしましょうか。

C. Person A suggests one thing and person B suggests another thing. Person A has no particular reason to disagree with B's suggestion. Follow the example.

Ex.　A's suggestion: to see a movie

　　　B's suggestion: to go to the zoo

　　　A: えいがを　みましょうか。

　　　B: それより、　どうぶつえんへ　いきましょうよ。

　　　A: どうぶつえん？

　　　B: いやですか。

　　　A: いいですよ。or　べつに。

1. A's suggestion: to eat a hamburger

　　B's suggestion: to eat sushi

2. A's suggestion: to go to the movies

　　B's suggestion: to watch T.V. at home

3. A's suggestion: to watch T.V.

　　B's suggestion: to listen to a new record

4. A's suggestion: to go to the library

　　B's suggestion: to go home

49

5. A's suggestion: to decide on only socks

    B's suggestion: to decide on socks and a handkerchief

6. A's suggestion: to study at Yoko's home

    B's suggestion: to study at the library

VI. EXERCISES

A. How would you:

1. greet a person on a nice day?

2. greet a person on a rainy day?

3. greet a person on a hot day?

B. Write a dialogue asking your date what he or she would like to do.

LESSON 12 *Jiro and Mary at the Zoo*

Situation: At the zoo

I. READING SELECTION

メリーさんと　じろうくんは　どうぶつえんへ　いきました。トムくんと

よう子さんも　どうぶつえんへ　いきました。

II. かいわ

じろう：　　ずいぶん　あるきましたね。　いま　なんじ？

メリー：　　十一時十分まえです。　ここで[1]　ちょっと　やすみましょう。

じろう：　　ああ、　のどが　かわいた。[2]　コーラを　のみましょうか。

メリー：　　ええ。

じろう：　　はい、　どうぞ。

メリー：　　ありがとう。　いただきます。あれは　トムさんじゃありませんか。[3]

じろう：　　あ、　そうですね。　トムくーん　こっちですよ。

トム：　　こんにちは、　こちらは[4]　よう子さんです。

よう子：　　はじめまして。

メリー：　　メリーです。　よろしく。

じろう：　　じろうです。　よろしく。

III. たんご

ずいぶん	a lot
あるきました（あるく）	walked. (Past tense of あるきます.)
十分	ten minutes
分	minutes
まえ	before; to
ちょっと	a little
ここ	here
やすみましょう（やすむ）	let's rest
ああ	oh
のどが　かわいた	✷ I'm thirsty. (かわいた　is the informal form of かわきました.)
かわいた（かわく）	become dry
はい、　どうぞ	Here, you are.
いただきます（いただく）	(Expression used when accepting something, or before eating or drinking.)
じゃありません	isn't; aren't
こちら（こっち）	this person here; this one of two or more; this way; hereabouts

51

よう子		(Girl's name.)	
はじめまして		(Expression used when meeting a person for the first time.)	

SUPPLEMENTARY VOCABULARY

えいがかん	movie theater	そこ	there
きっさてん	coffee shop	あそこ	over there

IV. ぶんぽう

1. <u>ここ</u>で　ちょっと　やすみましょう。　　　　　Let's rest here for a little while.

ここ belongs to a set of words called demonstratives and is used to point at or refer to a place. The ここ series:

ここ	area near the speaker
そこ	area near the listener
あそこ	area far away from the speaker and listener, but can be seen or is known to both
どこ	question word

2. ああ、のどが　<u>かわいた</u>　　　　　Oh, I'm thirsty.

かわいた is the informal past tense of the verb かわきます *to become dry*. The informal past tense of a verb is made by dropping the て from the -て form of the verb and replacing it with た or だ.

Ex.　かわいて　⟶　かわいた
　　　よんで　⟶　よんだ

3. あれは、トムさん<u>じゃありません</u>か。　　　Isn't that Tom?

じゃありません is the negative of です.

Ex.　あれは　トムさん<u>です</u>。　　　That's Tom.
　　　あれは　トムさん<u>じゃありません</u>。　That's not Tom.

4. <u>こちら</u>は　よう子さんです。　　　This is Yoko.

こちら *this person* is used when one is introducing someone. It corresponds to これ, as does そちら to それ and あちら to あれ. See lesson 7, grammar note 2.

V. DRILLS

A. Introduce your classmates to other classmates using the following example.

Ex.　トム：メリーさん、こちらは　よう子さんです。
　　　よう子：はじめまして。
　　　メリー：メリーです。　よろしく。

52

B. Answer the following questions in complete sentences.

    Ex. Q: どこで　たべますか。   Cue:　(McDonald's)

       A:　マクドナルドで　たべます。

     1. どこで　みますか。   (the movie theater)

     2. どこで　よみますか。   (the library)

     3. どこで　ききましたか。   (school)

     4. どこで　のみましたか。   (Mr. Tanaka's home)

     5. どこで　かいましたか。   (the department store)

C. Say the following in Japanese.

     1. Isn't that Mr. Akau?

     2. Isn't that Mr. Tanaka?

     3. Isn't that Tom's mother?

     4. Isn't that Mary's father?

     5. Aren't those new shoes?

     6. Isn't tomorrow a holiday?

D. Give negative answers for the following questions.

    Ex. Q: うちは　とうきょうですか。

       A: いいえ、<u>とうきょうじゃありません。</u>

     1.　あれは　としょかんですか。
       いいえ、

     2.　しけんは　あさってでしょう。
       いいえ、

     3.　これは　あたらしい　レコードですか。
       いいえ、

     4.　たんじょうびの　プレゼントですか。
       いいえ、

     5.　じろうくんは　はやおきですか。
       いいえ、

     6.　きょうは　デートですか。
       いいえ、

     7.　いい　おてんきですか。
       いいえ、

     8.　ひまですか。
       いいえ、

     9.　いやですか。
       いいえ、

VI. REVIEW

A. How would you say:

1. Let's rest at the coffee shop.
2. Let's eat a hamburger at McDonald's.
3. Let's read Japanese books at the library.
4. Let's drink coke at home.
5. Let's buy a birthday present at the department store.

VII. かんじ (Chinese characters)

A. Stroke order

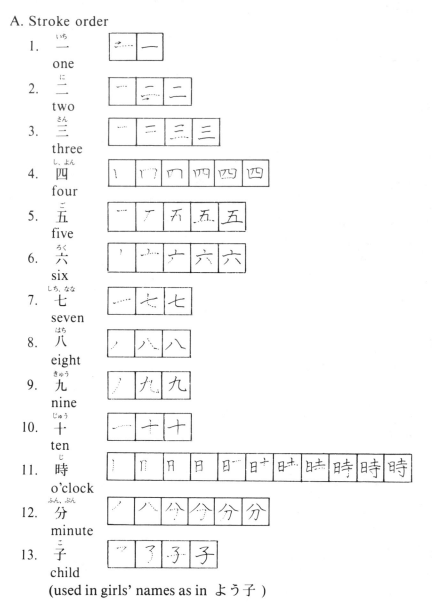

1. 一 (いち) one
2. 二 (に) two
3. 三 (さん) three
4. 四 (し、よん) four
5. 五 (ご) five
6. 六 (ろく) six
7. 七 (しち、なな) seven
8. 八 (はち) eight
9. 九 (きゅう) nine
10. 十 (じゅう) ten
11. 時 (じ) o'clock
12. 分 (ふん、ぷん) minute
13. 子 (こ) child
(used in girls' names as in よう子)

VIII. EXERCISE

Write a dialogue: Introduce Jiro Tanaka to your friends.

LESSON 13 *Lunch Time at the Zoo*

Situation: How to tell time and invite friends home.

I. READING SELECTION

おなかが　すきました。　もう　十二時半です。よう子さんの　うちは
どうぶつえんから[1]　ちかいです。よう子さんの　うちで　おひるを　食べます。
よう子さんの　うちは　ラーメンやです。

II. かいわ

じろう：　　ああ、おなかが　すいた。もう　十二時半ですよ。

トム　：　　もう　十二時半？[2]

じろう：　　おひるを　食べましょうよ。

よう子：　　じゃあ、うちへ　来ませんか。ははが　まっていますから。

メリー：　　わるいですねえ。[3]

よう子：　　いいえ、かまいません。ここから　ちかいですよ。

じろう：　　でも、おかあさんに　めいわくじゃありませんか。[4]

よう子：　　いいえ、ちっとも。うちは　ラーメンやですから。

III. たんご

おなかが　すいた	✶ I'm hungry. (すいた is the informal form of すきました.)
すいた　(すく)	become empty
十二時半	12:30
ちかい	near
ラーメンや	noodle shop
ラーメン	noodles
まっています	is waiting
わるいですねえ。	it is bad; it's not good; it's too much trouble
いいえ、かまいません。	It's no bother.
ここから	from here
…にめいわく	trouble to . . . ; inconvenience to . . .
ちっとも	not at all. (Used with negative verbs.)

SUPPLEMENTARY VOCABULARY

すぎ	past	ごぜん	A.M.
はん	half	ごご	P.M.

IV. ぶんぽう

1. ここから ちかいです。　　　　　　　　　　It's close from here.
   から after a noun means *from*.

2. Telling time.

   In Japanese, A.M. and P.M. come before the time.

   Ex. ごぜん十時　　　　　　　　　　　　　　10 A.M.
   　　ごご十時　　　　　　　　　　　　　　　10 P.M.

   分 means minutes and is used after the numbers designating hours. まえ *before; to,* and すぎ *past; after* are placed after 分 to mean *so many minutes before or after the hour.*

なんぷん	how many minutes	ろっぷん	6 minutes
いっぷん	1 minute	ななふん	7 minutes
にふん	2 minutes	はっぷん、はちふん	8 minutes
さんぷん	3 minutes	きゅうふん	9 minutes
よんぷん	4 minutes	じゅっぷん、じっぷん	10 minutes
ごふん	5 minutes		

   Ex.　9:15　　　九時十五分（すぎ）

   　　　8:45　　　九時十五分まえ

   　　　　　　　　八時四十五分（すぎ）　(fifteen to nine)

   It's 15 minutes to four.　　　　　　　四時十五分まえです。

   It's 15 minutes past nine.　　　　　　九時十五分すぎです。

   すぎ can be omitted, but まえ cannot.

3. わるいですねえ。　　　　　　　　　　　Literally, this means *It's bad, isn't it?*

   In Japanese culture it is proper etiquette to hesitate from accepting someone's offer. It is considered to be modest to refuse an offer at least once, and then consider accepting the favor.

4. おかあさんに めいわくじゃありませんか。　Isn't it troublesome to your mother?

   (Person)　にめいわくです　means　*it is inconvenient to (person).*

V. DRILLS

A. Construct a sentence using から with the words and phrases given in English.

   Ex.　Jiro; from Japan　　　　　　　じろうさんは　にほんから　きました。

   1. Mary; from school

   2. Yoko's home; from the airport

   3. the park; from my home

   4. the school; from here

B. Expansion: Complete the following with appropriate phrases.

   Ex. にほんから　来ました。

   1. がっこうから

   2. くうこうから

   3. うちから

C. Respond in a modest way to your friend's offer using
めいわくじゃありませんか。 or わるいですねえ。

   1. I'll take you to the airport.

   2. I'll give you a ride.

   3. Let's eat at my home.

   4. Let's have the party at my house.

   5. I'll take you home.

   6. You can have band practice at my house.

D. Answer the following using ちっとも in your response.

   Ex. おなかが すきませんか。　　ちっとも すきません。

   1. のどが かわきませんか。

   2. わかりますか。

   3. めいわくじゃありませんか。

   4. いやですか。

   5. きょうみが ありますか。

   6. おかねが ありますか。

E. Question-Answer: Use すぎ or まえ in your answer.

   Ex. Q: いま なん時ですか。　　　　　Cue: 5 to four

     A: 四時五分まえです。

1. 10 to eight	6. 4 to two
2. 5 after ten	7. 25 after nine
3. 15 to nine	8. 23 after three
4. 20 after four	9. 10 after five
5. 5 after seven	10. 7 to one

F. Say the following in Japanese.

   Ex. I come to school about 10 to eight.

     八時十分まえごろ がっこうへ 来ます。

   1. I go home about 4:40.

   2. I'll go to the library about 3:15.

   3. Please come about 9:30.

   4. I eat breakfast about 7:20.

   5. I ate lunch at about 15 to two.

VI. EXERCISES

A. Rearrange the words and phrases into Japanese sentences.

   1. すいた、 おなか、 が

   2. か、 来ません、うち、 へ

   3. ちかい、 です、 から、 よ、 ここ

   4. それより、 へ、 いきましょう、 どうぶつえん、 よ

   5. じゃありません、 あれ、 は、 か、 トムさん

B. Complete each dialogue by filling in the blanks saying that you'll be a bother (to someone).

1. いしい：　ああ、おなかが　すいた。

　　あべ：　　うちへ　来ませんか。

　　いしい：　わるいですねえ。

　　あべ：　　いいえ、かまいません。

　　いしい：　でも　おかあさん＿＿＿＿＿＿＿＿＿＿。

2. たなか：　　ちちの　くるまで　いきましょうよ。

　　わたなべ：わるいですね。

　　たなか：　　かまいませんよ。

　　わたなべ：でも、おとうさん＿＿＿＿＿＿＿＿＿＿。

VII.　かんじ

1. 来ます、来る、来て
   come

一	ー	口	卆	束	来	来	来

2. 食べます、食べる、食べて
   eat

ノ	人	人	今	今	令	食	食	食	食

3. 半
   half

`	ゝ	ン	二	半	半

LESSON 14 *At Jiro's Home*

Situation: Coming home from a date.

I. READING SELECTION

じろうくんも　トムくんも　デートから　かえりました。　デートは
たのしかったです。　トムくんに　てがみが　来ています。　おかあさんからです。

II. かいわ

じろう：	ただいま
トム　：	ただいま。
おかあさん：	おかえりなさい。
じろう：	おかあさん、　つめたいものが　飲みたい。¹
おかあさん：	はい、　はい、　すぐ　もっていきますから…。
トム　：	ほんとうに　つかれたね。
じろう：	うん。　でも　たのしかった²ね。
おかあさん：	はい。* むぎちゃを　どうぞ。　あ、　アカウさん、　てがみが 来ていますよ。³
トム　：	ほんとうですか。
おかあさん：	はい。
トム　：	どうも。
じろう：	ガール・フレンドから？
トム　：	ざんねんでした。　ははからですよ。

III. たんご

たのしかった（たのしい）	was enjoyable
てがみ	letter
来ています（来ている）	has arrived; has come
ただいま	(Expression used to announce one's arrival.)
おかえりなさい	welcome home
つめたい	cold. (Never used to describe climatic conditions.)
もの	thing
すぐ	right away
もっていきます（もっていく）	to take (something)
ほんとうに	really; truly
つかれた（つかれる）	tired. (Informal form of　つかれました.)
うん	yup; yeh; yes
むぎちゃ	tea made from roasted barley. (Generally, it is served cold during the summer.)
*はい	here you are

どうぞ	please. (Used when offering something.)
どうも	thank you
ガール・フレンド	girlfriend
ざんねんでした	it was too bad; it was unfortunate
ステレオ	stereo

IV. ぶんぽう

1. When verbs which take objects are changed to the -たい form, the object marker を is often replaced with subject marker が and what was the object of the sentence becomes the subject.

    Ex. つめたいものを　のみます。　　　　　I'm going to drink something cold.

    つめたいものが　のみたい。　　　　　I want to drink something cold.

    The formal form of the - たい form is made by adding です .

    Ex. いきます。　　　　　　　　　　　　I am going.

    いきたい。　　　　　　　　　　　　I want to go. (informal)

    いきたいです。　　　　　　　　　　I want to go. (formal)

2. たのし<u>かった</u>。　　　　　　　　　　(It) was enjoyable.

    In Japanese adjectives inflect and thus can be expressed in the past tense. It is generally formed by dropping the last syllable い of the nonpast form of the adjective and adding かった .When です is added it makes the statement formal.

    Ex. たのし ✕

    たのし＋かった＝たのしかった。　　　(informal)

    たのしかったです。　　　(formal)

    There is one exception, and that is the adjective いい *good* which has another form よい . The latter form よい is used in the inflection or conjugation of いい .

    よ ✕

    よ＋かった＝よかった

3. てがみが　<u>来ています</u>。　　　　　　A letter came (and is here).

    The -て form of motion verbs like　いく、くる、かえる　plus います are used to indicate a state resulting from a previous action or event.

    Ex.　トムさんは　としょかんへ　行っています。

    Tom (went and) is at the library (now).

    ちちは　かえっています。

    Father (came home and) is home (now).

V. DRILLS

A. Change the following adjectives to the past tense.

    Ex. たのしい ⟶　　たのしかった

1. あたらしい	6. あかい
2. ちかい	7. いい
3. たかい	8. あつい
4. おいしい	9. つめたい
5. おもしろい	10. ふるい

       (Use the adjectives listed in introductory units 6-8.)

B. Give the Japanese equivalent for the following.

1. The movie was good.

2. Yesterday was cold.

3. The sushi was good.

4. The book was interesting.

C. Substitution

1. コーラ が 飲みたい。
   おちゃ
   みず
   つめたいもの
   あついもの

2. ハンバーガー が 食べたいです。
   おすし
   ラーメン
   ケーキ
   ポテト・フライ

3. やすい ラジオが かいたい。
   おもしろい ほん
   おおきい くるま
   くろい くつ
   いい ステレオ

VI. EXERCISES

A. Write a dialogue for each of the following situations.

1. asking for a date

2. asking to go to a movie

3. parents asking about school

B. Select the appropriate situation for each of the following dialogues from the list given after each one.

1. もり： あついですね。
   おか： そうですね。
   もり： きょうは どこにしましょうか。
   おか： うみへ 行きましょうか。
   もり： いいですね。
   a. meeting at school on a rainy day
   b. meeting a friend on a hot day
   c. meeting a teacher after school

61

2. トム:　　　　はやく、　はやく。　でんしゃに　おくれますよ。

じろう:　　　すぐ　行きますから。　あ、　でんわ。

トム:　　　　ははが　いますから。

じろう:　　　でも。

トム:　　　　はやく　行きましょう。

トム:　　　　いってまいります。

じろう:　　　いって　まいります。

a. rushing out of school

b. rushing out of a restaurant

c. rushing out of the house

VII. かんじ

1. 飲みます、　飲む、　飲んで
   drink

2. 行きます、　行く、　行って
   go

LESSON 15 *At the Department Store*

Situation: Meeting someone unexpectedly at the department store.

I. READING SELECTION

じろうくんは　二かいの　おてあらいへ　行きました。　トムくんは
行きたくない[1]から　待っていました。　そこで　トムくんは　メリーさんと
よう子さんに　あいました。　メリーさんと　よう子さんも　デパートに
来ていました。

II. かいわ

じろう：　　　ちょっと　すみませんが、　おてあらいは　どこですか。

てんいん：　二かいに　あります。

じろう：　　　どうも。

トム：　　　　ぼくは　行きたくないから、ここで　待っています。

じろう：　　　じゃあ、　これを　見ていてください。

トム：　　　　はやくしてよ。

Mary sees Tom as he is waiting for Jiro.

メリー：　　　あ、　トムさん、　買いものですか。

トム　：　　　ええ。　じろうくんも　いっしょですが、おてあらいへ　行きました。

メリー：　　　よう子さん、　こっちですよ。

よう子：　　　あ、　トムさん、　こんにちは。　たくさん　買いましたね。

トム　：　　　これは　ぜんぶ　じろうくんの　買いものですよ。

よう子：　　　ほんとう？

III. たんご

二かい	second floor
かい	(Counter for floors.)
行きたくない	don't want to go
待っていました	was waiting
に　あります　（ある）	is located; (something) exists
ちょっと　すみませんが	excuse me, but . . . (Expression used when request-ing something.)
見ています　（見ている）	be watching
はやくして　（ください）	(please) hurry
いっしょ	together
たくさん	a lot; plenty (in quantity)
ぜんぶ	all (quantity)

SUPPLEMENTARY VOCABULARY

なんがい	what floor?
とこや	barber shop
レストラン	restaurant
ぎんこう	bank
ゆうびんきょく	post office
ゆうびんポスト	mailbox on the street
バスてい	bus stop
えき	railway station
ほんしゅう	Honshu, main island of Japan
ほっかいどう	Hokkaido, northernmost island of Japan
さっぽろ	Sapporo, capital of Hokkaido
きゅうしゅう	Kyushu, southern island of Japan
しこく	Shikoku, one of the four main islands, east of Kyushu
富士山	Mt. Fuji, the highest and the most famous of Japan's mountains
あそ山	Mt. Aso, active volcano on the island of Kyushu
パーキング ちゅうしゃじょう	parking
やっきょく	drug store
コーヒー・ショップ	coffee shop

IV. ぶんぽう

1. ぼくは　行き<u>たくない</u>から、　ここで　待っています。

I don't want to go, so I'll wait here.

いきたくない is the negative of いきたい and is formed by dropping the last syllable い and adding くない.

The negative of verbs in the - たい form has two possible formal forms:

Ex. いきたい

行きたくない。	I don't want to go. (informal)
行きたく { ないです / ありません	I don't want to go. (formal)

Ex. うみへ　行きたいです。	I want to go to the beach.
うみへ　行きたくない(です)。 うみへ　行きたくありません。	I don't want to go to the beach.

V. DRILLS

A. Ask the location of the following places beginning with the expression ちょっと　すみませんが。

Ex. ちょっと　すみませんが、　おてあらいは　どこですか。

64

1. library
2. telephone
3. bank
4. mailbox
5. bus stop

B. Give the Japanese equivalent for the following.
1. Tomorrow is a holiday, but I'm going to school.
2. These are cheap shoes, but they are good.
3. I am busy today, but I have time tomorrow.
4. I want to buy a typewriter, but I do not have money.
5. Yoko is going, but Mary is not going.

C. Question-Answer
Ex. Q: とうきょうは　どこに　ありますか。　　Cue: ほんしゅう
A: ほんしゅうに　あります。

1. ふじさんは　どこに　ありますか。　　　　　　ほんしゅう
2. あそざんは　どこに　ありますか。　　　　　　きゅうしゅう
3. さっぽろは　どこに　ありますか。　　　　　　ほっかいどう

D. Change the following to the informal form.
Ex. はやくしてください。　　はやくして。
1. 見てください。
2. よんでください。
3. しずかに　してください。
4. はやく　食べてください。
5. ちょっと　待ってください。
6. はやく　かえってください。
7. くうこうへ　行ってください。
8. ここに　いてください。

E. Change the following into the negative.
Ex. a. コーラが　飲みたいです。

b. コーラは　飲みたく $\begin{cases} ないです。 \\ ありません。 \end{cases}$

1. ハンバーガーが　食べたいです。
2. おおきい　くるまが　買いたいです。
3. つめたいものが　飲みたいです。
4. せいぶげきが　見たいです。
5. はやく　おきたいです。
6. どうぶつえんへ　行きたいです。

VI. EXERCISE

Review lessons 10 to 15, write dialogues similar to each of the lessons. You will find that the dialogues you have written can become one script. Form a group of two or three people and combine your scripts into one brief play. Then perform your play for the class.

VII. かんじ

1. 待ちます、 待つ、 待って
   wait

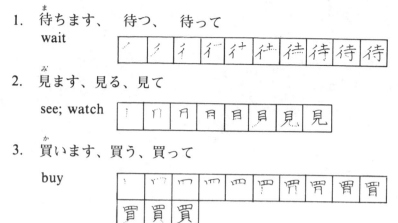

2. 見ます、見る、見て

   see; watch

3. 買います、買う、買って

   buy

66

LESSON 16 *Caught in the Rain*

Situation: Waiting for the rain to stop.

I. READING SELECTION

雨が　ふっています。　トムくんと　じろうくんは　かさが　ありませんから
こまりました。雨は　どしゃぶりです。　待っていますが、なかなか　やみません。

II. かいわ

じろう　：　　あ、　雨ですよ。　いやんなっちゃうな。[1]

トム　：　　どしゃぶりですね。

じろう　：　　ちょっと　待ちましょう。

トム　：　　うん。ああ、のどが　かわいた。コーラか　なにか[2] 飲みましょうよ。

じろう　：　　よく　コーラを　飲みますね。

トム　：　　いいじゃない (か)。[3]

じろう　：　　なかなか　やみませんね。　こまったなあ。

トム　：　　どうしました？　またトイレ？　じゃあ、タクシーで　帰りましょうよ。

III. たんご

雨（あめ）	rain
雨（あめ）が　ふっています。	It is raining.
かさ	umbrella
どしゃぶり	downpour
なかなか	not easily. (Used with negative verbs.)
やみません	won't stop
いやんなっちゃうな	I hate it! What a pain!
よく	often
…か　なにか	. . . or something
いいじゃない	that's all right, isn't it?
こまったなあ	Oh, darn!　(こまった is the informal of こまりました .)
どうしました	what happened? what's the matter?
トイレ	toilet
タクシー	taxi
帰りたい	want to return home

SUPPLEMENTARY VOCABULARY

かきました	wrote
こたえてください　（こたえる）	Please answer.
まだ	still, yet

IV. ぶんぽう

1. いやに　なっちゃう<u>な</u>。　　　　　　　　　How disgusting!

   な or なあ is often added to a statement that expresses the speaker's emotion and is directed to the speaker himself rather than to the listener even though it is audible to the listener.

   なっちゃう　is a contraction of　なってしまう　*something completed* and implies that one is vexed about what has happened. Here, Jiro is unhappy that it is raining.

2. コーラ<u>か　なにか</u>　飲みましょうよ。　　　　　Let's drink a coke or something (like that).

   <u>か　なにか</u>　*or something like that* is used to state a fact or suggest something.

   Ex. すしか　なにか(を)　たべましょう。　　　Let's eat sushi or something.
   　　ざっしか　なにか(が)　あります。　　　There is a magazine or something like that.

3. いいじゃない<u>か</u>。　　　　　　　　　　　It's okay!

   <u>か</u> is a sentence particle added to a statement in an informal or familiar conversation. The expression is used by male speakers when agreement is expected or when the speaker is displeased at what the listener has just said.

V. DRILLS

A. Substitution

1. <u>コーラ</u>か　なにか　飲みましょう。
   おちゃ
   ミルク
   みず

2. <u>ハンバーガー</u>か　なにか　食べましょう。
   おすし
   ポテト・フライ
   アイス・クリーム

B. Give the Japanese equivalent for the following.

1. It is raining. What a pain!
2. I came by car.
3. I spoke (to him) by telephone.
4. I wrote with a pencil.
5. Please answer in (by means of) Japanese.

VI. EXERCISES

A. Describe the situation after reading each dialogue.

1. わたなべ：　　よくふりますね。
   ブラウン：　　うん、きょうも　あさから…。
   わたなべ：　　ハワイも　雨が　よく　ふりますか。
   ブラウン：　　ええ、よく　ふりますよ。

68

2. あらかき：　　コーラか　なにか　飲みましょう。
　　さとう　：　　よく　コーラを　飲みますね。
　　あらかき：　　いいじゃないか。
　　さとう　：　　だめですよ。
　　あらかき：　　じゃあ、　みずを　飲みますよ。

3. アキナ　：　　はやく、　はやく。　クラスに　おくれますよ。
　　さかもと：　　まだ　はやいです。
　　アキナ　：　　でも…。
　　さかもと：　　いいですよ。

B. Create a dialogue in which you and a friend disagree on something.

VII. かんじ

1. 雨
   rain

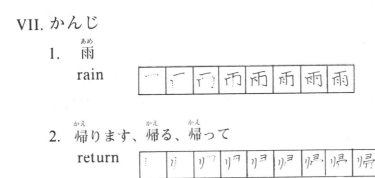

2. 帰ります、帰る、帰って
   return

LESSON 17 *After Returning Home from Shopping*

Situation: At home.

I. READING SELECTION

じろうくんと　トムくんは　買いものから　帰りました。じろうくんは　たくさん
買いものを　しましたが、　きみ子ちゃんに　おみやげを　買いませんでした。
でも　トムくんは　おみやげを　買いました。　きみ子ちゃんは　とても
よろこびました。

II. かいわ

じろう	:	おかあさん、　インスタント・ラーメン　つくってよ。
おかあさん	:	そんなに　おなかが　すいているの？[1]
トム	:	おひるを　食べませんでした[2]から。
おかあさん	:	しょうがない人たちねえ。
きみ子	:	じろうにいさん、　これなあに？　　見せて。
じろう	:	だめだめ。　おまえに　かんけいないよ。
トム	:	はい、　これ、　きみちゃんに。
きみ子	:	わあ、　おみやげ？　サンキュー。　だから　トムさん　好きよ。
じろう	:	トムくん（は）　きみ子に　あまいからね。

III. たんご

…ちゃん	(Informal form of さん attached to first names of children.)
おみやげ	present
とても	very
よろこびました	was happy
つくって (ください)	(please) make it
そんなに	to that extent
食べませんでした	did not eat
しょうがない	hopeless; pitiful; too bad
人 (ひと)	person
人たち	people
みせて (ください)	(please) show me
だめだめ	No!
おまえ	you. (Used for those younger than oneself.)
に	to; for (Particle.)
(お) にいさん	older brother
かんけいない	none of your concern

70

わあ	oh, boy!	好き	like
だから	that is why	あまい	sweet

SUPPLEMENTARY VOCABULARY

きらい	dislike	あに	my older brother

IV. ぶんぽう

1. そんなに　おなかが　すいている<u>の</u>?   Are you that hungry?

   The dictionary form plus の at the end of a sentence may replace the -ます form plus か in conversation with familiar persons.

   Ex. おなかが　すいていますか。   Are you hungry?

   おなかが　すいている<u>の</u>?

   これを　食べますか。   Will you eat this?

   これを　食べる<u>の</u>?

2. 食べ<u>ませんでした</u>。   I didn't eat.

   -ませんでした is the past tense of the nonpast negative -ません. To make the negative past add でした to the nonpast negative.

V. DRILLS

A. Write out the dictionary form of the following verbs: 行きます —→ 行く

   1. 来ます
   2. 帰ります
   3. 買います
   4. 食べます
   5. します
   6. よみます
   7. 飲みます
   8. 見ます
   9. はなします
   10. かきます
   11. ききます
   12. います
   13. あります

B. Change the following to the conversational form. Refer to introductory units for the verb list.

   Ex. おなかが　すいていますか。—→ おなかが　すいているの?

   1. 食べますか。
   2. これを　買いますか。
   3. もう　帰りますか。
   4. このほんを　よみますか。
   5. てがみを　かきますか。
   6. ビールを　飲みますか。

C. Change the following to the negative past tense.

Ex. 食べません ──→ 食べませんでした

1. 飲みません

2. 買いません

3. ほんを　よみません

4. てがみを　かきません

D. Give the Japanese equivalents for the following verbs using the different forms shown in the example.
Cue: to eat （食べる）

Ex. I will eat.　　　食べます。

I won't eat.　　　食べません。

Let's eat.　　　食べましょう。

Please eat.　　　食べてください。

I ate.　　　食べました。

I didn't eat.　　　食べませんでした。

1. to see　　　（みる）

2. to go　　　（行く）

3. to buy　　　（買う）

4. to read　　　（よむ）

5. to return　　　（帰る）

6. to write　　　（かく）

7. to speak　　　（はなす）

VI. EXERCISE

Give an appropriate Japanese expression for each of the following situations.

1. Tom and Jiro come running into the house, soaked from the rain. Mom asks why they didn't wait until the rain stopped. Jiro says that he is hungry. Exasperated, mom sighs and says:

2. Jiro receives a phone call from a friend. Kimiko pesters Jiro, wanting to know who it is. In disgust Jiro replies:

3. Tom wants a girl to go out with him, but he is too shy to ask her. When he finally works up enough courage to ask her out, he finds that the girl already has a boyfriend. To console him, Jiro says: (refer to lesson 14).

4. Jiro comes home from school in a bad mood. His teachers have assigned a lot of homework and tcsts. Jiro voices his complaint: (refer to lesson 16).

VII. かんじ

1. 人
   ひと
   people, person

2. 好き
   す
   like, prefer

72

LESSON 18 *Going for a Walk before Dinner*

Situation: Arguing and name calling.

I. READING SELECTION

ゆうしょくまで¹ じかんが ありますから、トムくんと じろうくんは さんぽを します。きみ子ちゃんと じろうくんは けんかを しました。 でも トムくんは きみ子ちゃんを いっしょに つれて行きます。

II. かいわ

トム ： ちょっと さんぽ しましょうよ。

じろう： うん、 ゆうしょくまで じかんが ありますからね。

トム ： きみちゃんも いっしょに 行きませんか。

じろう： おまえは うるさいから² だめ(です)！

きみ子： お母さん！

トム ： いいじゃないか。

きみ子： じろうにいさんの いじわる！

じろう： だから おまえは いやなんだ。

きみ子： お母さん！

III. たんご

ゆうしょく	dinner
まで	until
じかん	time
さんぽ	walk; stroll
けんか	fight
けんかを しました (けんかする)	fought
つれて行きます	to take (someone) along
さんぽしましょう	let's go for a walk
うるさい	a bother
いじわる	a meany
じろうにいさんの いじわる	You're mean, brother.
いやなんだ	I don't like it; I can't stand it.

SUPPLEMENTARY VOCABULARY

いくら	how much?
ひこうき	airplane
ドル	dollar

73

IV. ぶんぽう

1. ゆうしょく<u>まで</u>　じかんが　あります。　　　I have time until dinner.

まで is a particle which means *until* or *up to* a certain time, event, or place.

Ex. 十二時<u>まで</u>　ひまです。　　　　　　I'll be free until 12 o'clock.
　　ひるごはん<u>まで</u>　ここに　います。　I'll be here until lunchtime.

2. おまえは　うるさい<u>から</u>　だめ（です）。　　You are a bother, so you can't go.
　　　　　　　　　　　　　　　　　　　　　　　You can't go because you are a nuisance.

(Statement) から (statement). The statement which precedes から *so; therefore; because* gives the reason or cause for what is said in the statement following から.

Ex. 六時ごろ　行きます<u>から</u>、　待っていてください。

I will come around 6 o'clock, so please wait.

あしたは　やすみですから、うちに　います。

Because tomorrow is a holiday, I'll be at home.

V. DRILLS

A. Substitution
　　Ex. <u>ゆうしょく</u>まで　じかんが　あります。
　　Cue:　until supper

　　　1. class　　　　　　　　　　　　3. party
　　　2. lunch　　　　　　　　　　　　4. Japanese class

B. Complete the sentences using から.
　　Ex. 雨が　ふりますから、　うみへ　行きません。

　　　1. がっこうが　あります。
　　　2. おかねが　ありません。
　　　3. おひるを　食べませんでした。
　　　4. おまえは　うるさい
　　　5. にほんへ　行きたい

C. Substitution
　　1. Ex. <u>十二時</u>から　<u>三時</u>　まで　待ちました。
　　　　　　　　　(from)　　　(until)

　　　Cue:　12:00　　　　3:00

　　　1. 6:00　　　　　　　　　　　　　8:00
　　　2. day before yesterday　　　　today

　　2. Ex. ここから　デパートまで　バスで　行きました。

　　　Cue:　here　　　　　　department store

　　　1. here　　　　　　　　over there
　　　2. here　　　　　　　　park

3. home   school

4. library   post office

5. school   post office

VI. EXERCISE

A. Say the following in Japanese.

1. I can't stand it.

2. You're a bother.

3. What a pain!

4. I'm thirsty.

5. I'm hungry.

6. That's all right.

VII. かんじ

1. 母、（お）母さん
   mother

LESSON 19 *Father Returns Home from Work*

Situation: Preparing for dinner and welcoming dad home.

I. READING SELECTION

もう　そろそろ　お父さんが　帰ります。　お母さんと　おねえさんは　夕食の
じゅんびを　はじめます。

                 *   *   *

お父さんが　帰りました。　さきに　おふろに　入ります。　それから
おにいさんと　ビールを　飲みます。

II. かいわ

お母さん　　：　そろそろ　お父さんが　帰りますよ。

おねえさん：　じゃあ、　夕食の　じゅんびを　しましょう。

おにいさん：　ねえ、　ごはん　まだ？

おねえさん：　うるさいわねえ。

げんかんで

お父さん　　：　ただいま。

お母さん　　：　あ、　あなた、　お帰りなさい。

おねえさん：　お父さん、　さきに　おふろに　入ったら？[1]

お父さん　　：　そうだ[2]ね。

おにいさん：　お父さん、　ビールが　ひえていますよ。

お父さん　　：　そうか。[3]

III. たんご

そろそろ	soon; gradually
じゅんび	preparation
はじめます（はじめる）	to begin
げんかん	entry way to a Japanese home
じゅんびを　します	to prepare
じゅんびを　しましょう	let's prepare
さきに	first (of all)
入ったら（入ります）（入る）	why don't you go in?
おふろに　はいる	take a bath
わ	(Sentence final particle used by female speakers.)
あなた	you; dear. (Usually used by a wife to address her husband.)
それから	and then

76

そうだね	yes, may be
ひえています	is chilled
そうか	is that so; okay

SUPPLEMENTARY VOCABULARY

だいどころ	kitchen
いま	living room
しんしつ	bedroom
くすり	medicine
こたえる	to answer

IV. ぶんぽう

1. おふろに　入ったら？　　　　　　　　Why don't you take a bath?

   - たらどうですか　is used to suggest something or to give advice. In an informal situation, the ending clause　どうですか　is often omitted.

   The - たら form is made by adding - ら to the informal past.

   Ex.　入った ⟶ 入った<u>ら</u>

   行った ⟶ 行った<u>ら</u>

   食べた ⟶ 食べ<u>たら</u>

   がっこうに　行った<u>ら</u>？　　　　Why don't you go to school?

   おひるを　食べ<u>たら</u>？　　　　　Why don't you eat lunch?

2. そう<u>だ</u>ね。　　　　　　　　　　Yes, maybe.

   だ is the informal or plain form of です and is usually used by a male speaker in an informal situation.

   そうですね (formal)

   そうだね　　(informal)

3. <u>そうか</u>。　　　　　　　　　　　Is that so, okay.

   です is omitted in this expression. It is used usually by male speakers in an informal situation.

   そうですか (formal)

   そうか　　　(informal)

V. DRILLS

A. Give the formal form of the following phrases.

   Ex.　おふろに　入ったら？　　おふろに　入ったら　どうですか。

   1. がっこうに　行ったら？
   2. うちへ　来たら？
   3. くすりを　飲んだら？
   4. はやく　帰ったら？
   5. このほんを　よんだら？
   6. ひらがなで　かいたら？
   7. にほんごで　こたえたら？
   8. あたらしい　くつを　買ったら？

77

VI. REVIEW

A. Say the following in Japanese.

    Ex.   father's birthday   父の　たんじょうび

1. mother's car
2. older brother's girlfriend
3. Japanese car
4. Japanese language book
5. English book
6. American television

B. Substitution

1. Ex. にほんから

    Cue: Japan

    1. America
    2. school
    3. 3 o'clock
    4. here
    5. Hokkaido

2. Ex: ハワイまで

    Cue: Hawaii

    1. school
    2. 5 o'clock
    3. there
    4. bank
    5. railway station

3. Ex. うちから　がっこうまで

    Cue: home   school

    1. Hokkaido, Kyushu
    2. Tokyo, Honolulu
    3. Japan, Hawaii
    4. here, there
    5. 3 o'clock, 5 o'clock

C. Repeat Review Drill B.3 and complete the sentences with an appropriate verb.

    Ex. うちから　がっこうまで　くるまで　行きました。

VII. EXERCISES

A. Write a paragraph about each of the following.

    1. dating   3. going shopping

    2. going for a walk   4. going to a movie

B. Review the expressions, both in the dialogues and the introductory units. Write a dialogue using some of the expressions.

VIII. かんじ

1. 父、　（お）父さん
   father

2. 夕、　　　夕食
   evening　　dinner

3. 入ります、　入る、　入って
   enter

LESSON 20 *Planning for an Outing*

Situation: Family conversation

I. READING SELECTION

きょうは　土曜日です。　お父さんと　おにいさんと　トムくんは　ビールを
飲んでいます。　あしたは　五月五日で、[1] 子どもの日です。　お父さんも　休みだから
みんなで　ドライブに　行きます。お母さんが　おべんとうを　つくります。
きみちゃんだけは　ともだちの　パーティーに　行きますから、　ドライブに
行きません。

II. かいわ

トム	：	お帰りなさい。
お父さん	：	トムくん　いっぱい　どうですか。
トム	：	ビールですか。　すこし　いただきます。
じろう	：	ぼくも。
おにいさん	：	じろうは　だめ。　すぐ　ようから。
じろう	：	ねえ、　あした日曜(日)だね。　お父さんも　休みでしょう。
お父さん	：	うん。　どうして？
じろう	：	あした、　ドライブに　行きませんか。
お母さん	：	グッド・アイデア！
おにいさん	：	お母さん、　トムくんの　おかげで　英語が　じょうずに　なりました[2] ね。
お父さん	：	じゃあ、　お母さん、　べんとう　たのむよ。
お母さん	：	はい、　はい。
きみ子	：	きみ子も　行ってもいい？[3]
お母さん	：	きみちゃんは　あした　おともだちの　パーティーでしょう。
きみ子	：	つまんないな…。

（だいどころから）

おねえさん	：	夕食の　じゅんびが　できました[4] よ。

III. たんご

土曜日	Saturday
五月五日	May 5th
で	and
子どもの日	Children's Day. After World War II, May 5 was declared Children's Day, a national holiday.
みんなで	all together

ドライブ	drive; to go for a drive
（お）べんとう	packed lunch
つくります（つくる）	to make
（お）ともだち	friend
いっぱい	full; glassful
どうですか。	how is it? how about it?
すこし	a little
よう	get drunk
日曜日	Sunday
どうして	why?
おかげで	because of; thanks to
じょうず	skillful
に　なりました	became
たのむ（たのみます）	I'm counting on you. (Used when asking a favor.)
行ってもいい？	can I go? is it all right to go?
つまんないな	it's no fun; it's boring
できました	it's ready; it's completed

SUPPLEMENTARY VOCABULARY

きれい	pretty
へた	unskillful
ゆうめい	famous
いしゃ	doctor
スチュアデス	stewardess
なつ休み	summer vacation
ふゆ休み	winter vacation
こんがっき	this semester
なんにち	what day (of the month); how many days
月曜日	Monday
火曜日	Tuesday
水曜日	Wednesday
木曜日	Thursday
金曜日	Friday

IV. ぶんぽう

1. あしたは　五月五日<u>で</u>　子どもの日です。

Tomorrow is May 5th and it is Children's Day.

で *and* is the - て form of です　and connects two sentences to make one.

Ex. きょうは　五月五日です。
　　Today is May 5th.
　　きょうは　子どもの日です
　　It is Children's Day.

きょうは　五月五日で、子どもの日です。

Today is May 5th and it is Children's Day.

2. 英語が　じょうずに　なりました　　　　　You became skillful (good) in English. (Noun)

に　なりました *became*. The particle　に＋なる　follows a noun that indicates a goal, which in this case is to become good in English.

Ex. じろうくんの　おねえさんは　　　　　Jiro's older sister became a teacher.
　　せんせいに　なりました。

3. きみ子も　行ってもいい？　　　　　　　Can I (Kimiko) go too?

-て form + もいい　is the informal form of -ても　いいですか　and is used among peers and close friends. It is used to ask permission to do something.

Ex. おてあらいに　行ってもいいですか。　　May I go to the restroom?

きみ子も　行ってもいい？　　In a Japanese conversation, a child often repeats his own name when referring to himself. Here, きみ子　is referring to herself by using her own name.

4. 夕食の　じゅんびが　できました。　　　　　Dinner is ready.

(Noun)　が　できました　is used to mean *something (that is prepared) is ready*. The particle が＋できる　follows something that is made or prepared.

5. Months of the year

In Japanese the months of the year are expressed by adding 月 to the numbers 1 through 12.

Ex. 一月　二月　三月　四月　五月　六月　七月　八月　九月　十月　十一月　十二月

6. Days of the month

To express the days of the month .にち is attached to the numbers except for the days underlined below.

1st	ついたち	11th	じゅういちにち	21st	にじゅういちにち
2nd	ふつか	12th	じゅうににち	22nd	にじゅうににち
3rd	みっか	13th	じゅうさんにち	23rd	にじゅうさんにち
4th	よっか	14th	じゅうよっか	24th	にじゅうよっか
5th	いつか	15th	じゅうごにち	25th	にじゅうごにち
6th	むいか	16th	じゅうろくにち	26th	にじゅうろくにち
7th	なのか	17th	じゅうしちにち	27th	にじゅうしちにち
8th	ようか	18th	じゅうはちにち	28th	にじゅうはちにち
9th	ここのか	19th	じゅうくにち	29th	にじゅうくにち
10th	とおか	20th	はつか	30th	さんじゅうにち
				31st	さんじゅういちにち

V. DRILLS

A. Connect the following sentences using the -て form of です.

Ex. あしたは　五月五日です。　子どもの日です。
　　あしたは　五月五日で　子どもの日です。

1. これは　日本の　カメラです。　それは　アメリカの　カメラです。

2. これは　たなかさんの　あたらしい　くるまです。とても　いいです。

3. 日本語の　しけんです。　とても　むずかしいです。

B. Give the Japanese equivalent for the following in both the informal and formal forms.

<table>
<tr><td></td><td>Informal</td><td>Formal</td></tr>
<tr><td>Ex. Is it all right if I go?</td><td>行ってもいい？</td><td>行ってもいいですか。</td></tr>
</table>

    1. Is it all right if I come?

    2. Is it all right if I eat?

    3. Is it all right if I buy?

    4. Is it all right if I drink?

    5. Is it all right if I go home?

C. Give the Japanese equivalent using に　なる.

    Ex. He became good in Japanese.   日本語が　じょうずに　なりました。

    1. Mary became pretty.

    2. He became famous.

    3. I want to become a stewardess.

    4. I want to become a teacher.

    5. He became a doctor.

D. Give the Japanese equivalent using できました.

    1. Dinner is ready.

    2. Is the preparation for the party completed?

    3. The punch is ready.

    4. The homework is completed.

    5. Is lunch ready?

VI. かんじ

1. 日 (ひ、び、か、にち)

    day; Sunday

丿	冂	冃	日	日

2. 曜 (よう)

    day of the week

丶	刂	冂	日	日ㄱ	日ㄱ	日ㄱ	日ㄱㄱ	日ㄱㄱ	日ㄱㄱ
曜	曜	曜	曜	曜	曜	曜	曜	曜	

3. 休み (やす)

    holiday

丿	亻	仁	什	什	休	休

4. 英 (えい)

    English

一	一	艹	艹	苆	苂	英	英

5. 語 (ご)

    language, word

丶	亠	亠	言	言	言	言
訁	訮	話	語	語	語	語

6. 本 (ほん)

    book

一	十	才	木	本	本

83

7. 月 ^{かつ、げつ}

Monday; month; moon

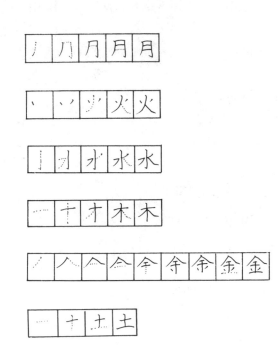

8. 火 ^か

Tuesday, fire

9. 水 ^{すい}

Wednesday, water

10. 木 ^{もく}

Thursday, tree

11. 金 ^{きん}

Friday, gold

12. 土 ^ど

Saturday, earth

APPENDIXES

SUMMARY OF GRAMMAR
LIST OF KANJI
LIST OF VERBS
GLOSSARY

SUMMARY OF　ぶんぽう

LESSON 1

1. Particles
2. たなか　じろうさん<u>の</u>　うち   (Noun) の (noun)
3. うち<u>は</u>　とうきょうです   (Noun) は (noun) です
4. うちは　とうきょう<u>です</u>   *is; am; are*
5. うちは　とうきょうです<u>か</u>   Question marker -
6. たなか　じろうです   Omission of the topic/subject
7. たなかさんは？   Omission of words other than topic/subject

LESSON 2

1. <u>きょう</u>　ひまですか   Time words
2. たなかさん<u>と</u>　アカウさん   Particle と
3. Word Order
4. うみ<u>へ</u>　いきます   Particle へ
5. いき<u>ます</u>   Nonpast formal form of verbs
6. いき<u>ませんか</u>   Verb negative + か
7. いいです<u>ね</u>   Particle ね
8. いき<u>ましょう</u>   Tentative form of verbs

LESSON 3

1. マクドナルド<u>で</u>　たべます   Particle で
2. おひる<u>を</u>　たべます   Particle を
3. おひるは？　<u>まだです</u>   *not yet*
4. Word Order: Topic/subject + location + action

LESSON 4

1. ごはんを　たべ<u>ました</u>   Formal past tense form of verbs
2. <u>いてください</u>   - てください　*please do*; - て form of verbs
3. ここ<u>に</u>　いてください   Particle に; に　います　versus に　あります
4. ぼく<u>が</u>　かいます   Particle が
5. ここに　いてください。　ぼくが　かいます<u>から</u>

        Particle　から

LESSON 5

1. えいが<u>に</u>　いきませんか   Particle に　+ motion verbs
2. なにを　みましょう<u>か</u>   *shall we . . . ?*
3. ちゃんばら<u>が</u>　いいです<u>か</u>、せいぶげき<u>が</u>　いいです<u>か</u>

        …か、…か
4. ちゃんばら<u>に</u>　<u>しましょう</u>   (Noun) に　します

LESSON 6

1. どうして　（だめですか）　　　　　　　Phrase deletion
2. しけん<u>が</u>　あります　　　　　　　Verbs　あります　and　います
3. しけんは　あさって<u>でしょう</u>　　　*isn't it?*
4. じゃあ、　がんばって　　　　　　　　Omission of　ください

LESSON 7

1. それは　<u>なん</u>ですか　　　　　　　なん　and　なに
2. これ／それ／あれ／どれ　　　　　　　*this/that/that over there/which*
3. くつしたと　ハンカチ<u>です</u>　　　です　—used in place of particle + verb
4. それ<u>だけ</u>ですか　　　　　　　　Particle　だけ

LESSON 8

1. そうです　versus　そうですね
2. うみへ　<u>いきたい</u>です　　　　　　-たい　form of verbs—used to express desire
3. <u>はやく</u>　あさごはんを　たべましょう　Adjectival and adverbial forms
4. <u>もう</u>　たべました　　　　　　　　*Already*

LESSON 9

1. でんしゃ<u>で</u>　いきます　　　　　　Particle　で　*by means of*
2. でんしゃ<u>に</u>　<u>おくれます</u>　　　Particle　に＋おくれます
3. でんしゃに　おくれます<u>よ</u>　　　　Particle　よ
4. さんぜんえん　あります　　　　　　　Quantity words
5. ぼく<u>も</u>　ごせんえん　あります　　　Particle　も
6. ろくじごろ　<u>でしょう</u>　　　　　　*probably*
7. ろくじ<u>ごろ</u>　　　　　　　　　　*about*

LESSON 10

1. なあに？　　　　　　　　　　　　　*What?*
2. Omission of　です／ですか
3. <u>ねえ</u>、おねえさん　　　　　　　Particle　ねえ
4. <u>しっています</u>か　　　　　　　　-て　form＋います—expresses action in progress or state of being
5. いい　えいがを　<u>やっています</u>　　やっています　*to perform, act, play*
6. おかね<u>が</u>　<u>かかります</u>　　　　が　かかります　*take time; take money*
7. おかねが　かかります<u>から</u>。　　　Particle　から　*because; since*

LESSON 11

1. どうぶつえんに　しました<u>が</u>、　ほんとうは　じろうくんは　あまり　きょうみが　ありません。
　　　　　　　　　　　　　　　　　(Statement)　が　(statement)
2. <u>それより</u>、　どうぶつえんへ　いき<u>ましょうよ</u>

　　　　　　　　　　　　　　　　　Giving an alternative suggestion

LESSON 12

1. ここ、そこ、あそこ、どこ   Demonstratives
2. ああ、のどが かわいた   Informal past tense of verbs
3. あれは トムさんじゃありませんか   じゃありません — negative of です
4. こちらは よう子さんです   こちら *this*

LESSON 13

1. ここから ちかいです   Particle から *from*
2. Telling time
3. わるいですねえ   Accepting an invitation
4. おかあさんに めいわくじゃありませんか   (Person)に めいわくです

LESSON 14

1. つめたいものが のみたい   (Object) が (Verb stem)たい form
2. たのしかった   Past tense for adjectives
3. てがみが 来ています   Use of -ています with verbs of motion

LESSON 15

1. ぼくは 行きたくないから ここで 待っています
     -たくない — negative of -たい form

LESSON 16

1. いやに なっちゃうな   Particle な / なあ
2. コーラか なにか 飲みましょうよ   か なにか *or something like that*
3. いいじゃないか   Particle か

LESSON 17

1. そんなに おなかが すいているの   Dictionary form ＋の
2. 食べませんでした   past tense of nonpast negative

LESSON 18

1. ゆうしょくまで じかんが あります   Particle まで
2. おまえは うるさいから だめ（です）   (Statement) から (statement)

LESSON 19

1. おふろに 入ったら   -たら form of verbs — used in giving suggestions or advice
2. そうだね   だ — plain form of です
3. そうか   Omission of です

LESSON 20

1. あしたは 五月五日で 子どもの日です   で *and*
2. 英語が じょうずに なりました   に なりました *became*
3. きみ子も 行ってもいい？   -て form + もいい — used in asking permission
4. 夕食の じゅんびが できました   が できました *is ready*
5. Months of the year
6. Days of the month

LIST OF KANJI

かんじ	Lesson	かんじ	Lesson
1. 子 （よう子）	12	22. 雨 （雨です）	16
2. 一	12	23. 帰 （帰ります）	16
3. 二	12	24. 人 （しょうがない人）	17
4. 三	12	25. 好 （好き）	17
5. 四	12	26. 母 （お母さん）	18
6. 五	12	27. 父 （お父さん）	19
7. 六	12	28. 夕 （夕食）	19
8. 七	12	29. 入 （おふろに入ります）	19
9. 八	12	30. 日 （日本）	20
10. 九	12	31. 曜 （日曜日）	20
11. 十	12	32. 休 （休み）	20
12. 時 （なん時）	12	33. 英 （英語）	20
13. 分 （十分）	12	34. 語 （英語）	20
14. 来 （来ます）	13	35. 本 （日本）	20
15. 食 （食べます）	13	36. 月 （月曜日）	20
16. 半 （十二時半）	13	37. 火 （火曜日）	20
17. 飲 （飲みます）	14	38. 水 （水曜日）	20
18. 行 （行きます）	14	39. 木 （木曜日）	20
19. 待 （待ちます）	15	40. 金 （金曜日）	20
20. 見 （見ます）	15	41. 土 （土曜日）	20
21. 買 （買います）	15		

LIST OF VERBS

- ます *Form*	*Dictionary Form*	-て *Form*	-た *Form*
あいます	あう	あって	あった
あけます	あける	あけて	あけた
あります	ある	あって	あった
あるきます	あるく	あるいて	あるいた
いいます	いう	いって	いった
いきます	いく	いって	いった
います	いる	いて	いた
いただきます	いただく	いただいて	いただいた
いれます	いれる	いれて	いれた
おきます	おきる	おきて	おきた
おくれます	おくれる	おくれて	おくれた
かいます	かう	かって	かった
かえします	かえす	かえして	かえした
かえります	かえる	かえって	かえった
かかります	かかる	かかって	かかった
かきます	かく	かいて	かいた
かわきます	かわく	かわいて	かわいた
ききます	きく	きいて	きいた
きこえます	きこえる	きこえて	きこえた
きます	くる	きて	きた
きを つけます	きを つける	きを つけて	きを つけた
こたえます	こたえる	こたえて	こたえた
こまります	こまる	こまって	こまった
します	する	して	した
しります	しる	しって	しった
すきます	すく	すいて	すいた
すみます	すむ	すんで	すんだ
たのみます	たのむ	たのんで	たのんだ
たべます	たべる	たべて	たべた
ちがいます	ちがう	ちがって	ちがった

つかれます	つかれる	つかれて	つかれた
つくります	つくる	つくって	つくった
つれます	つれる	つれて	つれた
とじます	とじる	とじて	とじた
なります	なる	なって	なった
ねます	ねる	ねて	ねた
のみます	のむ	のんで	のんだ
はいります	はいる	はいって	はいった
はじめます	はじめる	はじめて	はじめた
はなします	はなす	はなして	はなした
ひえます	ひえる	ひえて	ひえた
ふります	ふる	ふって	ふった
まちます	まつ	まって	まった
みえます	みえる	みえて	みえた
みせます	みせる	みせて	みせた
みます	みる	みて	みた
やすみます	やすむ	やすんで	やすんだ
やみます	やむ	やんで	やんだ
やります	やる	やって	やった
よいます	よう	よって	よった
よみます	よむ	よんで	よんだ
よろこびます	よろこぶ	よろこんで	よろこんだ
わかります	わかる	わかって	わかった
わすれます	わすれる	わすれて	わすれた
がんばります	がんばる	がんばって	がんばった
だします	だす	だして	だした
できます	できる	できて	できた

GLOSSARY

GLOSSARY

Arranged according to the Hiragana Syllabary

		Lesson
あ、	oh, hey	11
あいました	met	15
アイス・クリーム	ice cream	3
あおい	blue	IU 6, 10
あかい	red	IU 6, 6
あさ	morning	8
あさごはん	breakfast	8
あさって	day after tomorrow	2
あした	tomorrow	2
あそこ	over there	12
あそざん	Mt. Aso	15
あたらしい	new	IU 7, 6
あつい	hot	IU 7, 8
あなた	you; dear	19
あに	my older brother	10
あね	my older sister	10
あまい	sweet	17
あまり	not much. (Used with negative verbs.)	10
雨	rain	16
雨が ふっています	it is raining	16
アメリカ	America	6
ありがとう(ございました)	thank you	IU 5, 12
あります （ある）	to have	6
ありません	don't have	11
あれ	that one over there	7
あるきました	walked	12
いい	good	IU 6, 12
いい おてんきですね	it's a nice day, isn't it?	11
いいじゃない	that's all right	16
いいですね	sounds good	2
いいですよ	it's all right	11
いいえ	no	2
いいえ、かまいません	it's no problem	13
いいえ、べつに	no, not especially	5
いいます （いう）	to say	IU 5, 4

行きたい	I want to go	8
行きたくない	I don't want to go	15
行きましょう	let's go	2
行きます（行く）	will go	2
行きません	will not go	2
行きませんか	won't you go	2
いくら	how much?	18
いじわる	a meany	18
いしゃ	doctor	20
いす	chair	6
いそがしい	busy	5
いただきます（いただく）	(Expression used when accepting something, or before eating or drinking something.)	12
一	one	9
いっしょ	together	15
いっていらっしゃい	(Expression used when someone is leaving the house.)	12
いってまいります	I'll be going. (Used when you are leaving the house.)	IU 2, 9
行ってもいい	Can I go? Is it all right to go?	20
いっぱい	a glassful	20
いぬ	dog	IU 4
いま	now	2
いま	living room	19
います（いる）	to be	4
いやです	I don't like it	11
いやですか	Don't you like it? Do you find it unpleasant?	11
いやなんだ	I don't like it. I can't stand it.	18
いやんなっちゃうな	I hate it! What a pain!	16
いらっしゃいませ	Welcome!	IU 8
いれました	put in	9
インスタント・ラーメン	instant ramen	17
うち	home	IU 1, 1
うみ	beach; ocean; sea	IU 1, 2
うるさい	a bother	18
うん	yup; yeah; yes	14
え	oh?	8
ええ	yes	2

えいが	movie	IU 2, 5
えいがかん	movie theater	12
えい語	English language	IU 4, 6
えき	station	15
えん	yen	9
えんぴつ	pencil	IU 2, 6
へ	(Particle meaning *to* a place.)	2
おいしい	delicious	IU 6, 6
おおきい	big	IU 7, 14
お母さん	mother	8
おかえりなさい	Welcome home.	IU 3, 14
おかげで	because of	20
おかね	money	IU 4, 6
おきます（おきる）	to wake up	4
おくれます（おくれる）	to be late	9
おすし	sushi	IU 2, 5
おちゃ	green tea	IU 2, 11
おてあらい	restroom	IU 1, 2
おてんき	(good) weather	11
お父さん	father	7
おとうばん	monitor	8
おととい	day before yesterday	IU 5, 3
おなかが　すいた	I'm hungry	13
おねえさん	older sister	10
おねがいします	(Expression used when asking a favor.)	4
おはよう（ございます）	Good morning.	IU 1, 8
おひる	lunch	3
おふろ	bath	3
おまえ	you. (Used with peers or those who are younger.)	17
おみやげ	present	17
おもしろい	interesting	IU 8, 6
おやすみなさい	Good night.	IU 2
おんがく	music	IU 3, 5
か	(Particle.)	1
か　なにか	or something	16
かい	(Counter for floors.)	15
買います（かう）	to buy	3

買いもの	shopping	IU 2, 5
かいわ	dialogue	1
帰り	return	9
帰りたい	want to return	16
帰ります（帰る）	to return	4
かかります（かかる）	will take; cost	10
かがく	science	9
かきました	wrote	16
かきます（かく）	to write	4
かさ	umbrella	16
かたかな	(Japanese alphabet used for loanwords.)	IU 3
かていか	home economics	9
かまいません	It's no problem.	13
かみ	paper	IU 2, IU 6
カメラ	camera	6
火曜日	Tuesday	20
から	because; since	4
から	from	8
かわ	river	2
かわいた	dry; parched	12
かんけいない	It's none of your concern.	17
きを　つけて	Please be careful.	9
きいろい	yellow	IU 6
ききます（きく）	to listen; to hear	3
きっさてん	coffee shop	12
来ています	has arrived; has come	14
きのう	yesterday	IU 5, 3
来ました	came	13
来ます（くる）	to come	4
きゅうしゅう	Kyushu	15
きょう	today	IU 5, 2
きょうみ	interest	11
きらい	dislike	17
きれい	pretty	20
金曜日	Friday	20
九	nine	9
くうこう	airport	13
くすり	medicine	19

くださいい	please	15
くつ	shoes	IU 2, 12
くつした	socks	7
クラス	class	9
くるま	car	IU 2, 6
くろい	black	IU 6, 14
くん	(Masculine usage for さん.)	5
ケーキ	cake	3
けしごむ	eraser	6
けち	tightwad; cheapskate	10
けっこうです	no, thank you	IU 4
けんかを　しました	fought	18
けんかする	to fight	18
コーヒー・ショップ	coffee shop	15
コーラ	cola (coke)	4
こうえん	park	2
ここ	here	12
ここから	from here	12
ここに　いてください	Please stay here.	4
こたえてください	Please answer.	16
こたえる	to answer	15
こちら	this	12
こっち	over here	11
子どもの日	Children's Day	20
こまったなあ	Oh, darn!	16
こまりました	was troubled; don't know what to do	10
これ	this	7
これから	from now	5
こんがっき	this semester	20
こんにちは	Hello.	12
こんばんは	Good evening.	IU 1
さきに	first of all	19
サッカー	soccer	10
さっぽろ	Sapporo	15
さむい	cold	IU 7
さようなら	Good-bye.	IU 1
さん	(Suffix for people's names.)	1
三	three	9

そこ	there	12
それ	that	7
それから	and then	19
それだけ	that's all	7
それより	instead of that	11
そろそろ	gradually	19
そんなに	to that extent	17
‐たい	(Used to express desire.)	8
たいいく	physical education	9
タイプライター	typewriter	6
タオル	towel	9
たかい	expensive	IU 8, 14
たくさん	a lot; plenty (quantity)	15
タクシー	taxi	16
ただいま	(Used to announce one's arrival home.)	IU 3, 14
たなか	family name	1
たのしかった	was enjoyable	14
たのむ	I'm counting on you. (Used when asking a favor.)	20
食べたい	want to eat	8
食べました	ate	8
食べましょう	let's eat	11
食べます（食べる）	will eat	3
食べませんでした	did not eat	17
だめだめ	No!	17
タワー	tower	7
たんご	vocabulary	1
たんじょうび	birthday	7
ちいさい	small	IU 7
ちかい	near	IU 8, 13
父	my father	7
ちっとも	not at all. (Used with negative verbs.)	13
ちゃん	(Suffix for names.)	17
ちゃんばら	sword fighting in samurai movies	5
ちゅうしゃじょう	parking	15
ちょっと　しつれい	excuse me	IU 6
ちょっと　すみません	excuse me	15
ちょっと　待ってください	Please wait a moment.	15

にいさん	older brother	17
二かい	second floor	15
日曜日	Sunday	20
日本	Japan	IU 1, 2
日本語	Japanese language	IU 3, 4
ねえ、	(Address particle used to get someone's attention.)	10
ねこ	cat	IU 4
ねます（ねる）	to sleep; to go to bed	4
の	(Particle.)	1
ノート	notebook	6
のどが　かわいた	throat is dry; I am thirsty	12, 6
のみます（のむ）	to drink	3
のみもの	drinks	4
はい	here you are. (Used when offering something.)	14
はい、どうぞ	here you are. (Used when offering something.)	12
入ったら？	Why don't you go in?	19
入る	to enter	19
はじめまして	(Used when meeting a person for the first time.)	12
はじめます（はじめる）	to start	19
ハ	eight	9
はなします（はなす）	to speak	4
母	my mother	8
はやい	early	16
はやおき	early riser	8
はやく	quickly	8
はやくして（ください）	(Please) hurry up.	15
ハワイ	Hawaii	16
半	half past	13
ハンカチ	handkerchief	7
ハンバーガー	hamburger	4
ひえています	is chilled	19
ひこうき	airplane	18
人たち	people	17
ひま	free time	IU 4, 2
ひゃく	one hundred. (Counter for hundreds.)	9
ひらがな	hiragana	IU 3, 19

ふじさん	Mt. Fuji	15
フット・ボール	football	9
ふゆ休み	winter vacation	20
ふりました	rained	16
ふります（ふる）	to rain	16
ふるい	old	IU 7, 6
分	minutes	12
へた	unskillful	20
ほっかいどう	Hokkaido—northernmost Japanese island	15
ホノルル	Honolulu	1
本	book	IU 3, 17
ほんしゅう	Honshu—main Japanese island	15
ほんとう？	really?	15
ほんとうに	really; truly	14
ほんとうは	actually	11
まい日	every day	IU 5
まえ	before; to	12
マクドナルド	McDonald's	3
-ましょう	(Verb suffix to express *let's*.)	3
-ます	(Formal nonpast verb suffix.)	3
-ません	(Formal nonpast negative verb suffix.)	3
まだ	not yet; still	3, 16
待ちましょう	let's wait	16
待っています	I am waiting	13
まで	until	18
まん	ten thousand. (Counter for ten thousands.)	9
ミーティング	meeting	9
みじかい	short	IU 8
みず	water	IU 2, 14
みずうみ	lake	2
みずぎ	swimwear	9
見せてください	please show me	17
見ましょうか	shall we see . . .	5
見ます（見る）	to see	3
ミルク	milk	16
むぎちゃ	barley tea	14

むずかしい	difficult	IU 7, 20
めいわく	trouble; inconvenience	13
メリー	Mary	10
も	also; too	9
もう	already	8
木曜日	Thursday	20
もっていきます	to take (thing) along	14
もの	thing	14
やきゅう	baseball	10
やさしい	easy	IU 7
やすい	inexpensive	IU 8, 14
休みました	I rested	12
休みましょう	let's rest	12
休みます（休む）	to rest	4
やっきょく	drug store	15
やっています	is doing; is having; is playing	10
やま	mountain	2
やみません	won't stop	16
ゆうえんち	amusement park	2
夕食	dinner	18
ゆうびんきょく	post office	15
ゆうびんポスト	mailbox	15
ゆうめい	famous	20
よ	(Sentence ending particle used for emphasis.)	9
よう	get drunk	20
よう子	Yoko (Girl's name.)	12
よく	often	16
よみます（よむ）	will read	4
よろしく	How do you do.	1
よろこびました	was happy	17
四	four	9
よんでください	Please read.	IU 9
ラーメン	noodles	13
ラーメンや	noodle shop	13
ラジオ	radio	14
れきし	history	9
レコード	record	4
レストラン	restaurant	3

れんしゅう	practice	9
六	six	9
六時	six o'clock	9
は	(Subject/topic marker.)	1
わ	(Sentence final particle used by females.)	19
わあ	Oh boy!	17
ワイキキ	Waikiki	5
わかります（わかる）	understand	IU 4
わかりません	I don't understand	IU 9
わすれました	I forgot.	IU 9
わたくし	I; me (Both masculine and feminine.)	4
わるい	not good	13
が	(Subject marker.)	4
が	but. (Used to connect two statements.)	11
ガール・フレンド	girl friend	14
がっこう	school	IU 1, 2
がんばって	give it all you've got; hang in there	6
ぎんこう	bank	15
月曜日	Monday	20
げんかん	entry way to a Japanese home	19
ごご	P.M.	13
ごぜん	A.M.	13
五	five	9
語	language	20
五月五日	May 5th	20
ごちそうさま（でした）	Thank you for the meal.	IU 4
ごはん	meal; cooked rice	IU 2, 3
ごめんください	Excuse me. (Used when announcing oneself.)	IU 8
ゴルフ	golf	10
ごろ	approximately (time)	9
ざっし	magazine	6
ざんねんでした	too bad; it was unfortunate	4
時	(Counter for time.)	9
時かん	hour; time; period	2, 9
じゃありません	isn't; aren't	12

土曜日	Saturday	20
ドライブ	(go for) a drive	20
ドル	dollar	18
どれ	which	7
バス	bus	15
バスてい	bus stop	15
バスケット	basketball	9
バレーボール	volleyball	10
ビール	beer	17
びじゅつ	art	9
ビッグ・マック	Big Mac	4
ぶんぽう	grammar; structure	1
べつに	not especially	5
べんきょう	study	IU 2, 3
べんとう	box lunch	20
ぼく	I; me. (Masculine usage.)	4
パーキング	parking	15
パーティー	party	20
ピアノ	piano	9
プール	swimming pool	2
プレゼント	present	7
ペン	pen	6
ポテト・フライ	french fries	4

ABOUT THE AUTHORS

ESTHER M. T. SATO, professor of education in the College of Education at the University of Hawaii, teaches foreign language methods and coordinates the student teaching program for foreign language majors. For more than fifteen years, she has also served as the liaison officer between the Hawaii Department of Education and the private Japanese language schools.

MASAKO SAKIHARA has taught Japanese at the University of Hawaii and, since 1979, at the University of Hawaii High School.

LOREN I. SHISHIDO also taught at the university laboratory school, at both the elementary and secondary levels.

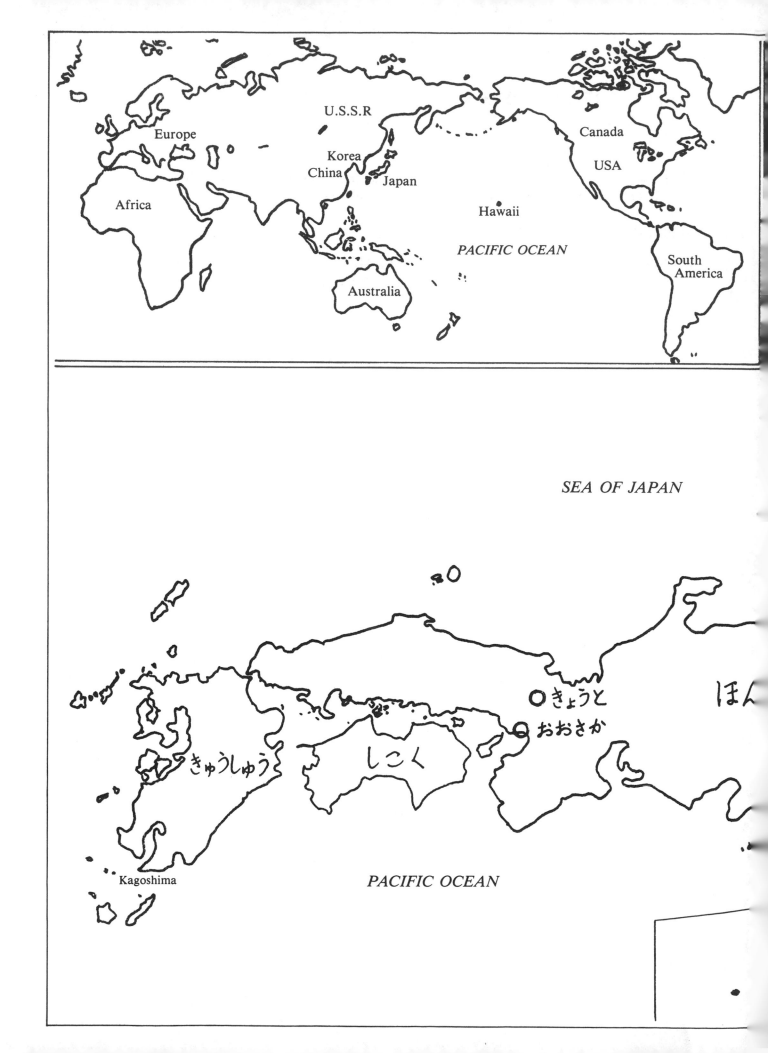

Europe

U.S.S.R

Korea
China
Japan

Africa

Canada

USA

Hawaii

PACIFIC OCEAN

South
America

Australia

SEA OF JAPAN

きょうと
おおさか

ほん

きゅうしゅう

しこく

Kagoshima

PACIFIC OCEAN

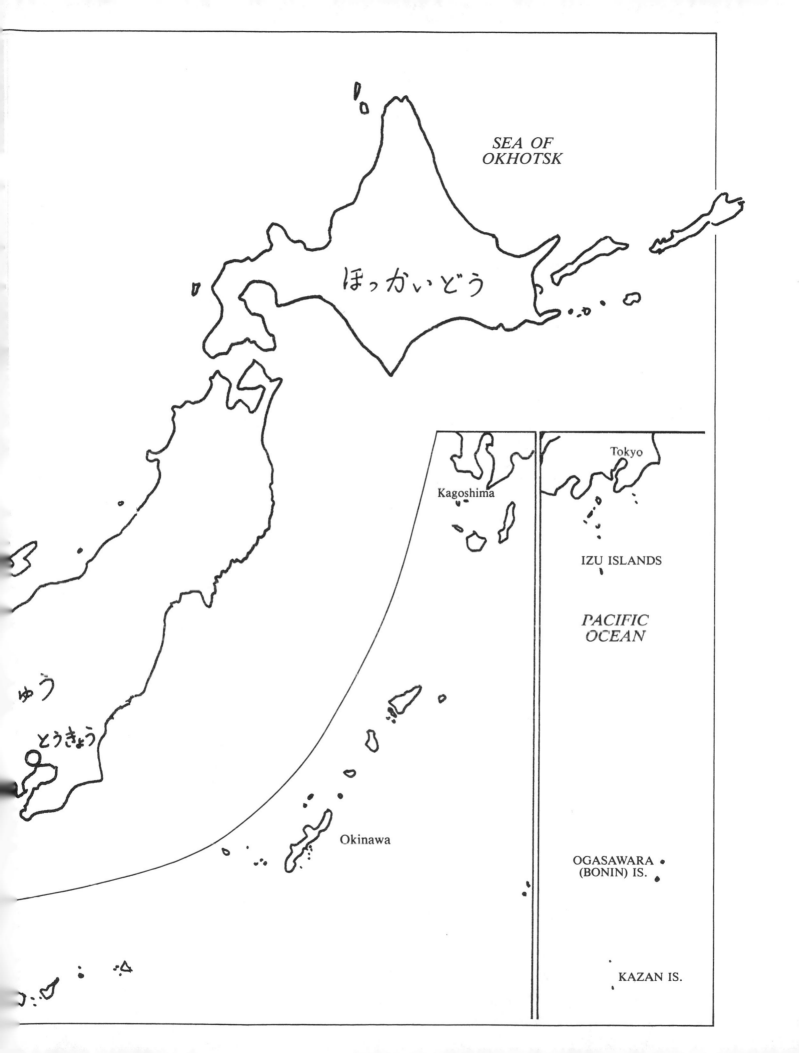

SEA OF
OKHOTSK

ほっかいどう

ゅう

とうきょう

Tokyo

Kagoshima

IZU ISLANDS

PACIFIC
OCEAN

Okinawa

OGASAWARA
(BONIN) IS.

KAZAN IS.

ごじゅうおん

ぱぎょう	ばぎょう	だぎょう	ざぎょう	がぎょう		わぎょう	らぎょう	やぎょう	まぎょう	はぎょう	なぎょう	たぎょう	さぎょう	かぎょう	あぎょう	
ぱ	ば	だ	ざ	が	ん	わ	ら	や	ま	は	な	た	さ	か	あ	あだん
ぱあ	ばあ	だあ	ざあ	があ		わあ	らあ	やあ	まあ	はあ	なあ	たあ	さあ	かあ	ああ	ちょうおん
パ	バ	ダ	ザ	ガ	ン	ワ	ラ	ヤ	マ	ハ	ナ	タ	サ	カ	ア	かたかな
ぴ	び	ぢ	じ	ぎ			り		み	ひ	に	ち	し	き	い	いだん
ぴい	びい	ぢい	じい	ぎい			りい		みい	ひい	にい	ちい	しい	きい	いい	ちょうおん
ピ	ビ	ヂ	ジ	ギ			リ		ミ	ヒ	ニ	チ	シ	キ	イ	かたかな
ぷ	ぶ	づ	ず	ぐ			る	ゆ	む	ふ	ぬ	つ	す	く	う	うだん
ぷう	ぶう	づう	ずう	ぐう			るう	ゆう	むう	ふう	ぬう	つう	すう	くう	うう	ちょうおん
プ	ブ	ヅ	ズ	グ			ル	ユ	ム	フ	ヌ	ツ	ス	ク	ウ	かたかな
ぺ	べ	で	ぜ	げ			れ		め	へ	ね	て	せ	け	え	えだん
ぺい	べい	でい	ぜい	げい			れい		めい	へい	ねい	てい	せい	けい	えい	ちょうおん
ペ	ベ	デ	ゼ	ゲ			レ		メ	ヘ	ネ	テ	セ	ケ	エ	かたかな
ぽ	ぼ	ど	ぞ	ご		を	ろ	よ	も	ほ	の	と	そ	こ	お	おだん
ぽう	ぼう	どう	ぞう	ごう			ろう	よう	もう	ほう	のう	とう	そう	こう	おう	ちょうおん
ポ	ボ	ド	ゾ	ゴ		ヲ	ロ	ヨ	モ	ホ	ノ	ト	ソ	コ	オ	かたかな

Katakana ちょうおん is expressed by '—' or '|'

For example, コーヒー； セーター； コーヒー セーター

Exceptions to ちょうおん

えだん：ええ；ねえ；おねえさん

おだん：おおきい；おおい；とおい；とおり；とおる；とお

Limited Usage

を is used only for the object particle in a sentence.

へ is pronounced え when used as a particle in a sentence.

は is pronounced わ when used as a particle in a sentence.

つ and ツ in small letters followed by か 、 た 、 ぱぎょう (row) are pronounced with a breath-stop and given one syllable length. However, when followed by さぎょう , there is no breath-stop, but the さぎょう sound is lengthened to two syllable lengths.

Ex. まって （たぎょう）

いっしょ （さぎょう）

In a compound word the じ sound is written ぢ when the original word begins with ち . Similarly, づ is used instead of ず when the original sound is つ .

づ is used for the ず sound when the preceding sound is つ in the same word. Similarly ぢ is used for the じ sound when the preceding sound is ち .

ぴゃ	びゃ	じゃ	ぎゃ	りゃ	みゃ	ひゃ	にゃ	ちゃ	しゃ	きゃ	
ぴゃあ	びゃあ	じゃあ	ぎゃあ	りゃあ	みゃあ	ひゃあ	にゃあ	ちゃあ	しゃあ	きゃあ	ちょうおん
ピャ	ビャ	ジャ	ギャ	リャ	ミャ	ヒャ	ニャ	チャ	シャ	キャ	
ぴゅ	びゅ	じゅ	ぎゅ	りゅ	みゅ	ひゅ	にゅ	ちゅ	しゅ	きゅ	
ぴゅう	びゅう	じゅう	ぎゅう	りゅう	みゅう	ひゅう	にゅう	ちゅう	しゅう	きゅう	ちょうおん
ピュ	ビュ	ジュ	ギュ	リュ	ミュ	ヒュ	ニュ	チュ	シュ	キュ	
ぴょ	びょ	じょ	ぎょ	りょ	みょ	ひょ	にょ	ちょ	しょ	きょ	
ぴょう	びょう	じょう	ぎょう	りょう	みょう	ひょう	にょう	ちょう	しょう	きょう	ちょうおん
ピョ	ビョ	ジョ	ギョ	リョ	ミョ	ヒョ	ニョ	チョ	ショ	キョ	